Democracy in Pakistan

Democracy in Pakistan

Crises, Conflicts and Hope for a Change

Ali Abbas Hasanie
Political scholar and analyst

authorHOUSE®

AuthorHouse™
1663 Liberty Drive
Bloomington, IN 47403
www.authorhouse.com
Phone: 1-800-839-8640

Published by AuthorHouse   04/26/2013

ISBN: 978-1-4817-9068-0 (sc)
ISBN: 978-1-4817-9113-7 (e)

This book is dedicated to the martyrs (shuhada) who sacrificed their lives in the ongoing fight against extremism and injustice, to preserve the very constitution this nation was built on.

Contents

1. Introduction

Acknowledgements ix

Foreword—Prof. Saeed Mirza, McGill University, Montreal xi

Foreword—Mdm. Louise Harel, Speaker National Assembly......... xiii

2. Pakistan

Democracy in Pakistan 1

3. Articles

Pakistan: a nation in search of a leader............................. 11

EDC is discriminating against overseas Pakistanis 18

Next general election is a test of people's power in Pakistan 21

Pakistan must adopt a National Unity Bill in parliament............... 30

Pakistan a democratic country without an official opposition in
parliament... 37

President must dissolve parliament immediately to appoint a
caretaker government... 43

SC's decision on dual nationals contradicts the fundamental
rights granted to citizens by constitution 49

Is time running out for free and fair elections in Pakistan?............. 51

Democracy under corrupt politicians is a fraud against people of
Pakistan 59

Dual nationality of Pakistanis does not contradict the constitution ... 65

From Islamabad bunker accord to Lahore MQ Secretariat
agreement... 69

4. Statements

ECP must allow Overseas Pakistanis to take part in
General Elections... 77

ECP grants overseas Pakistanis right to vote 79

Dual Nationality Bill in Pakistan is a step in right direction 81

SC not doing justice if they don't recognize rights of dual
national Pakistanis to be a parliamentarian 82

Overseas Pakistanis sorrow over SC verdict 84

ECP must find mechanism to set up polling stations abroad
    for Overseas Pakistanis 87
Expats may serve as polling officers, body of Canada-based
    Pakistanis tells ECP 88
OPF requests nation to offer salute to CJP and OAS 91
Overseas Pakistanis have constitutional right to take part in
    country's affairs 93

5. **Press Releases**
    Government must fulfill its reponsibility by providing safety
        and security to its citizens... 99
    Fakhruddin Ebrahim and his associates praised by OPF 101
    Criticism of Qadri by Pakistani politicians, media disappoints
        OPF 104

6. **Key Events in Pakistan**
    Pakistan—Key events in chronological order 109

Acknowledgements

Arguably, Pakistan is currently in a dire situation with a gloomy future. Sadly, it's perhaps one of the worst periods in Pakistan's history. The dismal condition is the most unfortunate and very discouraging. **Any hope to reform this situation is in the hands of our people**—*the voters*.

As a concerned Pakistani citizen, I felt obligated to share my personal thoughts and opinions on Pakistan's current state, in particular the upcoming elections, as well as suggest concrete and vibrant solutions to some of the problems that our country is up against.

This book in your hand is a collection of my writings that have been published in various newspapers in Pakistan and other countries. I felt compelled to write these articles and statements regarding the deplorable conditions in Pakistan as we witness it being damaged. Through these articles and statements I have offered some practical and compelling advice after having carefully studying and analyzing the current political affairs as well as the history of Pakistan along with its constitution and laws.

As sensible citizens, it is all of our responsibility to do our individual parts, be it via voting, raising a voice against any injustices, volunteering our services in a charitable organization or writing articles, towards creating a productive and just society.

"Indeed, Allah will not change the condition of a people until they change what is in Themselves." The Quran (13:11)

The founding Fathers of Pakistan had a certain vision, which they initiated. It is now our duty, and the duty of every generation thereafter, to further implement that vision and to take it to the next level. This is not only for the sake of Pakistan, its future as well its position in the world, but also for the dreams and hopes of every child that is born in Pakistan. We all have the right to live in a just society with the basic amenities to prosper and fulfill our dreams while giving back to the society that nurtures us.

"My message to you all is of hope, courage and confidence. Let us mobilize all our resources in a systematic and organized way and tackle the grave issues that confront us with grim determination and discipline worthy of a great nation."
Quaid-e-Azam Muhammad Ali Jinnah

I am grateful to Professor Saeed Mirza, McGill University, Montreal, Canada, and Madam Louise Harel, former Speaker of the National Assembly of Quebec, for taking time to write a Foreword for this book. I am thankful to Mr. Abdul Aziz Khan for his encouragement to my writings as well his valuable suggestions and editing of my articles. I am also thankful to Mr. Hasan Rizvi for his valuable input and editing of my work. My thank also goes to Mr. Abis Hussain for his support of my work and his assistance in distributing my published articles to overseas readers. I am deeply thankful to Ms. Syeda A. Zehra for colleting all the articles, statements and press releases that had accumulated over the many months and compiling them into a book form. A special mention to my wife Meraj for all her patience, understanding and support over the many years as I did my small part and strove towards improving the future of Pakistan through my active participation in the affairs of Pakistan and Pakistanis, and through my articles, research and meetings both at home and abroad.

I dedicate this book to the future of Pakistan. I would love to receive the comments and suggestions from the readers not only on this book itself but also on Pakistan, the elections, the current conditions and its future.

I hope this humble contribution towards our Nation will make a positive difference and open the eyes of those politicians and bureaucrats within the government who are working against the progress, development, system and the future of Pakistan while trampling the hopes and aspirations of millions of Pakistanis.

With that, I leave you with a quote from Albert Einstein for you to ponder over.

"The world will not be destroyed by those who do evil, but by those who watch them without doing anything"

God bless Pakistan and keep its citizens safe and secure with a bright, dynamic and prosperous future.

Foreword

The author must be commended for his frank, insightful, objective and thorough analysis of the recent history of turmoil in Pakistan, along with a detailed historic review of the early years after independence.

Mr. Ali Abbas Hasanie examines and explains the differences between the electorates in several developed countries and Pakistan, where the masses are relatively uneducated, poor and depend entirely for food and shelter for their families on their "masters" or "lords". He argues that these people are ill-informed politically and are coerced to vote for "them and their political parties". The author notes that on August 11, 1947, Quaid-e-Azam Muhammad Ali Jinnah, the first Governor General of Pakistan, had declared that Pakistan's constitution would be based on the guiding principles of "an inclusive and impartial government, religious freedom, rule of law and equality for all". These principles were subsequently adopted and elaborated by the Constituent Assembly on March 12, 1949. The prevailing situation in Pakistan is contrary to these guiding principles. Mr. Hasanie raises a very pertinent question: "What has happened to Pakistan in its 65 year history?"

The book contains 12 articles, authored by Mr. Hasanie, which deal with varied subjects, including national leadership, Parliament, national unity, plutocracy (instead of democracy), people's power, roles of the government and the opposition (which is non-existent for reasons elaborated by the author), individuals with dual nationality, justice and the Supreme Court, and corruption and fraud. He has argued strongly with 8 statements focusing principally on granting of voting rights to individuals with dual citizenship of Pakistan and another country, because of the strength, stability and prosperity these individuals would bring to Pakistan. His recent press releases on behalf of the Overseas Pakistanis Federation (OPF) have emphasized the government's responsibility for safety and security of all citizens, and the concerns of OPF about the voting rights of individuals with dual citizenship.

All of the articles, statements and press releases constitute a passionate and perhaps a controversial plea by the author, and his sincere desire to change the course of Pakistan's politics and reorient the country to the principles enunciated by the Quaid-e-Azam in August 1947. Whether the reader agrees or disagrees with the author, he has correctly emphasized that the approaching general election would be a test of Pakistan's peoples power by examining the prevailing mode of governance and the performance of the various leaders and their political parties, before exercising their valuable vote.

Finally, Mr. Hasanie quotes Albert Einstein who stated: "The world will not be destroyed by those who do evil, but by those who watch them without doing anything". The author contends that presently most Pakistanis are simply watching the current situation without doing anything. He urges the people of Pakistan to exercise their vote to ensure that in future all Pakistanis are safe and secure, and to guarantee a bright and prosperous future for their children and grandchildren.

Saeed Mirza
Professor Emeritus,
McGill University, Montreal, Canada

Foreword

I am delighted to offer my thoughts on the book "Democracy in Pakistan: Crises, Conflicts and Hope for a Change" written by Mr. Ali Abbas Hasanie. Ali and I first met in a Pakistan community meeting in Montreal on the eve of Pakistan Independence Day a few years ago. We quickly became good friends as we both strived for the betterment of ethnic communities in Montreal. Cricket was the second reason. Ali and I worked together numerous times to provide space and facilities to the South Asian communities wishing to play their favourite sport; this has reinforced our friendship.

I quickly realized that Mr. Hasanie is strongly involved in his community. He works with various NGOs engaged in social, cultural, sports and human rights affairs. He also served on the boards of directors of various provincial and national organizations including the Pakistan Association of Quebec, where he also worked as President, and the Overseas Pakistanis Forum. He currently serves as the Chairman of the Action Committee for racial profiling of Pakistanis in Canada, focusing on the defense of human rights. It is therefore not surprising that Mr. Hasanie is so well-known in the South-Asian communities of Montreal; his contribution towards the well-being of the community is highly commendable.

Mr. Hasanie is not only a human rights advocate, he is also an accomplished political scholar and analyst who regularly writes about the Pakistani political situation. His writings have been published in various newspapers both in Pakistan and abroad. They cover a wide range of issues faced by his home country including corruption, poverty, unemployment and violence. Yet, they strive to offer advices and words of wisdom to the people of Pakistan to improve the future of their country. Mr. Hasanie's book also calls upon the Pakistani diasporas to stay involved in the consolidation of Pakistan's democracy, including Canadian citizens of Pakistani origin and descent. Such a message contributes to strengthening the relationship between Quebec and Canada and Pakistan.

I am pleased to see Mr. Hanasie's articles, statements and press releases compiled in the form of a book; they will provide its readers greater insight into the political history of Pakistan, its problems and opportunities. With the next general elections approaching, such a book was indeed needed.

I offer my admiration and gratitude to Mr. Hasanie. His work is an honest contribution to the progress of Pakistan's democracy. I wish his voice will stay strong in the years to come, as he strives towards improving the future of Pakistan.

Louise Harel
Leader of the Official Opposition City of Montreal
Former Speaker of Quebec National Assembly

Democracy in Pakistan

The creation of Pakistan was the result of a movement for a separate homeland for the Muslims of undivided India. This movement began with the birth of All India Muslim League on December 30, 1906 and concluded when Muslims gained independence on August 14, 1947 (27 Ramadan 1366). This movement was initially started to protect the Muslim minority amid fears of neglect and under-representation in case the British decided to grant local self-rule. It further evolved when Dr. Sir Muhammad Iqbal called for an autonomous state for Muslims in 1930 and Quaid-e-Azam Muhammad Ali Jinnah, the head of All India Muslim League, espoused the *Two Nation Theory* by adopting the Lahore Resolution in 1940 to demand the formation of an independent state for Muslims. In June 1947, the national leaders of British India, including Jawaharlal Nehru and Abul Kalam Azad representing the Congress, Muhammad Ali Jinnah representing the Muslim League and Master Tara Singh representing Sikhs, agreed to the terms of transfer of power and independence with the British rulers.

Pakistan, the sixth most populous state with a population of 180 million, falls into a region which was historically ruled by numerous empires and dynasties including the Indian Mauryan Empire, the Persian Achaemenid Empire, the Arab Umayyad Caliphate, the Mongol Empire, the Mughal Empire, the Durrani Empire, the Sikh Empire and the British Empire. This region decided to form democratic states after the independence movement began. The vision of Muslim state was given by the father of nation Quaid-e-Azam Muhammad Ali Jinnah in his address to the constituent assembly as *"an inclusive and impartial government, religious freedom, rule of law and equality for all"*. The Objective Resolution of 12th March, 1949, gave the framework of a Pakistan Constitution by declaring that the constitution Pakistan will be based on principles of democracy, freedom, equality, tolerance and social justice as enunciated by Islam.

Pakistan is the second largest Muslim country in the world after Indonesia. Pakistan has the seventh largest standing armed forces in the world. Pakistan has Nuclear power as well as nuclear weapons. Pakistan is a member of the United Nations, Commonwealth and the Organization of Islamic

1

Cooperation. Pakistan's post independence history has been characterized by the various periods of military rules, instability and conflicts confrontations within and with neighboring India especially over Jammu and Kashmir. The country continues to face challenging problems including illiteracy, poverty, religious extremism, corruption and terrorism.

Pakistan adopted its first constitution nine years after its independence on March 23, 1956, that dissolved the Dominion and replaced it by the Islamic Republic of Pakistan. Two years later, this constitution was suspended when the military took control of the country under first Martial Law in 1958. The constitution was replaced first by Basic Democracy Ordinance of 1959 and then by the 1962 Constitution, which transformed the parliamentary form of government into the presidential form of government labeled by some political analysts as the representational dictatorship. Amidst allegations during the 1960s that the economic development and employment opportunities favored West Pakistan, there was a nationwide uprising in Bengali nationalism and independence movement in East Pakistan.

The 1962 Constitution was dissolved and the military general Mohammad Yahya Khan took over the government under the second Martial Law in 1969. In a highly controversial election in 1971, a West Pakistan dominated political party came to power and a new constitution based on a parliamentary form of government was adopted in 1973. This constitution remained as the basic script of rule during all civilian and military regimes since 1973 with desired amendments of the government of the day.

The first democratic era from 1947 to 1958 faced two major conflicts, i.e., the regional disparity between West and East Pakistan, and the power play for sharing powers between the Governor General/President and the Prime Minister. After Quaid-e-Azam Muhammad Ali Jinnah, who dominated both the Governor General and Prime Minister positions, the controversy over power-sharing is said to have played a major role in the assassination of Liaquat Ali Khan, the second most powerful politician after Quaid-e-Azam in Pakistan. This period recorded continuous dismissals and forced resignations of six Prime Ministers. General Mohammad Ayub Khan, the Commander-in-Chief of the Pakistan army, then took over the power and dismissed the civilian Prime Minister and dissolved the Parliament.

The second democratic era from 1971 to 1977 was completely dominated by Zulfiqar Ali Bhutto and his democratically elected government of Pakistan People's Party (PPP) and their socio-economic policies. Pakistan adopted its new 1973 Constitution, which was unanimously passed by the democratically elected parliament. This constitution gave absolute power to Prime Minister and the Parliament with only a ceremonial role given to the President as head of the state. Zulfiqar Al Bhutto became the Prime Minister on August 14, 1973 while Chaudhri Fazal Elahi became the President. The government nationalized all major industries and the healthcare and educational institutions, which led to economic stagnation and disaster. Pakistan became the leader in Islamic world and Pakistan launched its first nuclear program to be on par with India. Lieutenant General Gul Hasan was appointed as the Chief of Army Staff but was dismissed from his post after he refused the order to suppress the police strike. General Tikka Khan then became the Army Chief and upon his retirement, General Zia-ul Haq was made the Chief of the Army Staff. East Pakistan became a separate country called Bangladesh. The Government dropped all charges against Mujibur Rehman, the leader of the Awami League (East Pakistan), and released him from house arrest while recognizing the newly created country of Bangladesh. Federal Security Forces, set up by Z. A. Bhutto, aggravated the political opponents, which caused major civil disorder and unrest in the country. Following the secession of East Pakistan, the call for an independent Baluchistan grew immensely causing severe political instability and unrest. Z.A. Bhutto sacked two provincial governments within six months, arrested two chief ministers, two governors, forty four MNAs and MPAs, banned National People's Party and charged those responsible with high treason.

Z.A. Bhutto called the general elections in 1977 where PPP won the election by a wide margin. Opposition led by Pakistan National Alliance (PNA) alleged wide spread vote rigging and major violence escalated across the country paralyzing the normal life in Pakistan. Major General K.M. Arif, loyal to Z.A. Bhutto, advised him that an army coup was in the planning. Z.A. Bhutto held a meeting with PNA that culminated into an agreement to form a government of national unity, dissolving the parliament and calling for fresh elections. General Zia-ul Haq, chief of army staff, ignored the agreement and imposed martial law with Z.A. Bhutto being deposed and arrested. Later the Lahore High Court convicted him with the murder of his opponent. He was hanged in Rawalpindi jail in April 1979.

The third democratic era started upon the culmination of the military regime of General Zia-ul Haq who got killed in a plane crash in August 1988. It was largely believed to be a western conspiracy after the Afghan *mujahedeen* drove Russia out of Afghanistan. Benazir Bhutto, the daughter of Z.A. Bhutto returned to Pakistan in April of 1986 after being in self-exile for seven years. Ghulam Ishaq Khan succeeded General Zia-ul Haq as President and called general elections in November of 1988. Eight political parties formed an Islamic Jamhuri Ittihad (IJI) with the help of establishment under the leadership of Mian Nawaz Sharif. Pakistan People Party won the elections and Benazir Bhutto was sworn in as the first woman Prime Minister of Pakistan on December 2, 1988. Her government was subsequently dissolved by the President on charges of wide-range corruption and misuse of power.

New general elections were held in October 1990, and IJI won 104 seats with only 45 seats won by Pakistan Democratic Alliance (PDA) that included PPP. Nawaz Sharif became the Prime Minister on November 6, 1990. He started having conflicts with the army and as a result, General Asif Nawaz replaced General Mirza Aslam Beg as army chief. In May 1993, President Ghulam Ishaq Khan dismissed Nawaz Shariff as Prime Minister on the charges of corruption. His decision was challenged in the Supreme Court, which restored the National Assembly and Prime Minister Nawaz Sharif. The President however did not abide the court decision. On the interruption of Pakistan army, both President Ghulam Ishaq Khan and Prime Minister Nawaz Sharif resigned.

The new elections were called in which PPP won 86 seats and PML-Nawaz won 72 seats. Benazir Bhutto became the Prime Minister for the second time and PPP managed to get Farooq Lagari elected as President. General Asif Nawaz was replaced by general Jahangir Karamat as Chief of Army Staff and Chairman of Joint Chief of Staff Committee. In a major scuffle between Asif Ali Zardari, the husband of Benazir Bhutto, and Mir Murtaza Bhutto, a politician and brother of Benazir Bhutto, Murtaza Bhutto got assassinated in Karachi. President Laghari sacked Benazir Bhutto as Prime Minister and dissolved the parliament on the charges of corruption and crimes.

With new elections were held in February 1997, Nawaz Sharif and his party received 2/3 majority by winning 135 seats. Nawaz Sharif was sworn in as Prime Minister. With 2/3 majority in Parliament, Nawaz Sharif acted as an absolute dictator. The Parliament amended the constitution and stripped the President of all his constitutional power to make him a ceremonial President. When his elected members started switching sides, he brought forward an amendment to the constitution again called "horse trading and *lotacracy*" banning the practice of switching sides by the members of parliament which the Chief Justice rejected. Nawaz Sharif later developed a severe tussle with the judiciary over the appointment of judges and was charged with contempt of court. With 2/3 majority in Parliament, Nawaz Sharif amended Pakistan's

Contempt of Court law by providing the right of appeal and suspending the conviction while the appeal was being heard in the court. President Laghari refused to sign this amendment and the country was driven into a major constitutional crises. Nawaz Sharif intended to impeach President Laghari on his refusal to sign the amendment. The proceeding of the impeachment was halted when the army stepped in to mediate between the Prime Minister and the President.

Nawaz Sharif's supporters stormed the Supreme Court during the court proceeding on contempt. A major scuffle ensued with the judiciary who called the army for the protection of the Supreme Court. Nawaz Sharif established special courts, against the Chief Justice's advise, to benefit his allies and supporters, which eventually proved to be a humiliating blot on the face of the justice system of Pakistan. President Farooq Laghari was forced to resign in December 1997. Pakistan conducted a nuclear test in May 1998 and Nawaz Sharif chaired the meeting of the Deference Committee of the Cabinet (DCC). The Army Chief, a four star general and a veteran of the army, General Jahangir Karamat disagreed with Nawaz Sharif and stressed the re-creation of National Security Council (NSC) instead of DCC. Nawaz Sharif banned opening of new foreign exchange accounts in Pakistan and suspended all withdrawal of foreign exchange, which developed a controversy with overseas Pakistanis account holders.

The Lahore Declaration was signed by Nawaz Sharif and A. B. Vajpayee, Indian Prime Minister, which did not mention the dispute of Kashmir. This was not appreciated by the army. Nawaz Sharif dismissed general Jahangir Karamat, which was not liked by the army. General Pervez Musharraf was appointed as Chief of Army Staff. Nawaz Sharif also dismissed Admiral Fasih Bukhari as Chairman of Joint Staff and appointed Pervez Musharraf instead. Pakistan obtained supremacy in Kargil war against India but Nawaz Sharif agreed to end the war upon the advice of the USA against the wishes of Pakistan army. Nawaz Sharif developed a major altercation with the Judiciary and the Army.

Nawaz Sharif enhanced his confrontation with General Pervez Musharraf and his army men and while he was planning to sack General Pervez Musharraf from the position of Chief of Army Staff, the military generals ousted Nawaz Sharif instead from power and placed him under house arrest. Later Nawaz Sharif was convicted of hijacking and terrorism and sentenced to life imprisonment. He later went into exile to Saudi Arabia. The third military era started with General Pervez Musharraf as President and Chief of Army Staff.

The fourth democratic era started in February 2008 when General Pervez Musharraf and his government agreed, under the advise of the USA, on the return of both Benazir Bhutto and Nawaz Sharif to Pakistan by waiving their charges to participate in the elections called for February 2008. After an unsuccessful attempt on her life upon arrival, Benazir Bhutto was assassinated before the elections. The people of Pakistan in an attempt to bring the change in government voted for both PPP (124 seats) and PML-N (91 seats) while incumbent party PML-Q received only 54 seats. PPP initially formed the government with the alliance of PML-N and ANP (13 seats) but later PML-N decided to sit in the opposition in parliament and left the alliance. PPP then formed a new alliance with PML-Q, MQM and ANP, and governed the entire five years of a democratically elected parliament. Major amendments to the constitution were made to strip President of all his powers. General Pervez Musharraf resigned as President in August 2008 and Asif Ali Zardari of PPP got elected as President in September of 2008.

In February of 2009 the government conceded to Taliban and announced a truce with them by accepting a system of Islamic law in Swat valley, which was boycotted by a member in the government alliance. This agreement later caused a major confrontation between the government and Taliban as the Pakistan army had to launch the operation *Rah-e-rast* to clear Swat valley of the Taliban. The extremist groups gained power during this regime and there was a sharp rise in sectarian and political killings, bombing and *bhatta-khori* (ransom), which resulted into massive killings including the killing of Punjab governor Salman Taseer and minorities minister Shahab Bhatti. The confrontation between the government, army and judiciary stepped up resulting into the Memogate scandal and the conviction of the Prime Minister in contempt of the Supreme Court. The unrest increased in the provinces of Baluchistan, Sindh and Khyber Pakhtunkhwa resulting into an increase in the suicide bombing and terrorism activities across these provinces.

Peace and security in the country became a major issue as people suffered the worst shortages of food, gas, electricity, employment and sharp rises in the cost of living. The Pakistani rupee lost its exchange value substantially and businesses have started to leave the country. Government borrowing soared substantially and the country reached to the verge of bankruptcy. While politicians praised themselves for completing the term of a democratically elected parliament, the reality shows as masses are fed up and simply want to change the government. The instability in the country has reached to its peak while political parties blamed each other for destruction to gain votes in the next elections. The parties that are not in the parliament are gaining popularity. Dr. Tahir-ul Qadri, a popular cleric and head of a political party, lodged a severe campaign and a long march against the corruption and corrupt electoral system in Pakistan.

The government signed an accord with Dr. Qadri and promised a neutral interim Prime Minister and major electoral reforms before the polls. The Parliament has completed its five years term and the elections have been announced for May of 2013.

It is quite evident from the analyses that it is not the system of democracy that is at fault but it is the incompetent, dishonest, corrupt and power hungry bunch of politicians who made the mockery of the democratic system in the country for their own personal benefits and ego. Pakistan was created with the sacrifices of hundreds of thousands of lives and as of today these sacrifices are still being given by the victims of terrorism, extremism and the injustices.

Pakistan was built on the pillars of Faith, Unity and Discipline. Faith means the faith in God, faith in humanity, faith in honesty and faith in justice. Unity means the unity through peace, unity through tolerance and unity through love. The discipline means the discipline of law and order, the discipline of respect and moral values, and the discipline of peaceful living and brotherhood.

Pakistan has fertile lands, water, resources, nuclear power and above all the honest, educated and skilled people who can run an honest democratic system for the well being of its people today and beyond. The power is in the hands of the voters. We must put aside our personal preferences, religious and linguistic alliances and regional and *biradery* commitments to give a fair chance to those honest and capable leaders who can build our country on honesty, fairness and justice and bring it to the next level as envisioned by its founders.

We have a dream—let us fulfill that dream and elect the honest and capable candidates in the upcoming election. And the HOPE is that we all can bring about a change in 2013 and beyond for better.

Articles

Pakistan: a nation in search of a leader

Is Pervez Musharraf a better option amongst politicians of today?

On Tuesday, November 9, 1982 at the Queen Elizabeth Hotel, Montreal, Canada when I took the podium as President of Pakistan Association of Quebec and urged the army general Zia-ul Haq that he must restore the democracy in Pakistan, a crowd of over 1,000 Pakistanis in the hall applauded on my voice and shouted back to support my demand at a public meeting chaired by General Zia-ul Haq, the President of Pakistan, and me on his visit to Canada.

In response to my demand, General Zia-ul Haq made a speech citing reasons for delaying the process of democracy in Pakistan; I was quite stunned that the charged up crowd of 1,000 people calmed down and bought the arguments against the democracy in Pakistan, why? Because, General Zia-ul Haq told the crowd that democratically elected governments of the past were *elected dictators* who, under the façade of democracy, were committing atrocities against Pakistan and the innocent people of Pakistan. He said the people of Pakistan were victims in the cruel hands of elected *jagirdar* (landlords), *sanatkar* (major industrialists), *tribal chiefs* and the *bourgeois* who controlled the livelihood of weak, poor and working class such as *kisan* (farmers) and *mazdoor* (labourers) in their electoral regions who had no option but to vote for their masters. General Zia-ul Haq told that Pakistan was being targeted by the external forces (same situation exists today) who were looking to destroy Pakistan's nuclear program; and in such an environment the security of our land was far above the demand of the people for democracy; the democracy which in his opinion was a recipe to destabilize Pakistan and to install the rule of corrupt politicians and corrupt and incompetent bureaucrats.

Ali Abbas Hasanie addressing a crowd with General Zia-ul Haq seated left, Montreal, Canada. Photo courtesy of Pakistan Association of Quebec Montreal.

What is a Democracy? A democracy is a system of government that is generally practiced in a free world; however, its paradigm and application differ from one country to another. In countries such as Britain, the United States, Germany, France or Japan where masses are educated, economically well off and socially free from all kinds of coercion, the process of free and fair elections is much different than in the countries, for example Pakistan, where the masses are not that educated, where the masses are poor and directly dependent for their livelihood upon those who contest in the elections; the situation of voters becomes more grave due to (a) social pressure from the society to avoid confrontation against the rich and powerful who can cause personal damages to voters and their families both financially and otherwise, and (b) the state patronage and intimidation to influence the election results to the likings of ruling parties. This phenomenon gave rise to an environment in which a large percentage (about 60%) of impartial and fair minded people do not participate into the voting process while the bias and socially pressured voters take up the polls to cast fair and unfair votes to the party and candidates of their choice. This is the democracy in Pakistan.

The political history of our nation began in 1906 with the birth of All India Muslim League in undivided India. Later a call from Sir Mohammad Iqbal in 1930 for a separate state for Muslims, perpetuated by Quaid-e-Azam Muhammad Ali Jinnah's Two Nation Theory at the Lahore Resolution of March 23, 1940, gave birth to a new nation called Pakistan on August 14, 1947 However, the dilemma faced to this newly created state was the formation of a constitution for a land with six distinct cultures and languages i.e., Punjabis,

Bengalis, Sindhis, Mohajirs (Urdu speaking immigrants from UP, Bihar and other parts of undivided India) Baluchees and Pathans.

Knowing the gravity of cultural and linguistic diversity along with religious implications, Quaid-e-Azam Muhammad Ali Jinnah, the first Governor General of Pakistan, on August 11, 1947 declared the guiding principles for a constitutional frame work i.e., "an inclusive and impartial government, religious freedom, rule of law and the equality for all". These principles were further clarified and adopted by the Constituent Assembly under the Objective Resolution of 12th March, 1949 which proclaimed the basic elements of constitution that Pakistan would be a federation in which the fundamental rights of citizens shall be guaranteed, where the judiciary shall be independent, where Muslims will be able to lead their lives according to Quran and *Sunnah*, where minorities will freely profess and practice their religion and culture; all the above under the umbrella of principles of democracy, freedom, equality, tolerance and social justice. The question we ask ourselves today, did it happen in 64 years of history of Pakistan after independence?!

Today, Pakistanis a free nation; but do you think that the people of Pakistan enjoy the fundamental rights under the principles of equality, religious freedom and the rules of law and social justice? In 64 years of Pakistan's history, the country was ruled by two forces i.e. civilian regimes and the military regimes. The 32 years of civilian regimes, lead by democratically or non-democratically elected governments, gave us governments of four (4) governor generals, none of them were directly elected, nine (9) presidents, perhaps only two of them were directly elected and eighteen (18) prime ministers including caretakers only six of them directly elected by the people Of these civilian regimes, people can only remember four (4) leaders who served with some prominence and legacy and that include Quaid-e-Azam Muhammad Ali Jinnah (Governor General), Liaqat Ali Khan (Prime Minister), Sir Khuwaja Nazimuddin (Governor General and Prime Minister), and Zulfiqar Ali Bhutto (President and Prime Minister). Zulfiqar Ali Bhutto's legacy was to unite and lead the Islamic world and to initiate the nuclear program in Pakistan; but he is also known to bring the nationalization program which destroyed the economic and social systems; and the patronage and corruption of his government which put the safety of the country in danger. Apart from these leaders, people can not forget the two other elected civilian prime ministers in recent past namely Begum Benazir Bhutto and Mian Nawaz Sharif whose regimes were so incompetent and corrupt that in spite of the fact that they were elected in polls twice, their own civilian presidents sacked them both times Mian Nawaz Sharif, after being pardoned for his crimes, is once again back into the political arena in a hope to become the Prime Minister knowing full well the poor and dismal record of his governance with acute corruption and undisputed incompetence of past two times of his elected government. The BBC ran a documentary on his mass corruption in June of 1999 in England while he was a sitting prime minister. This documentary is still available today in the archives of BBC.

The 32 years of army regimes were imposed on the people of Pakistan in military coups as a result of mass corruption of the civilian governments that brought the stability and safety of Pakistan in danger. This situation ultimately encouraged the army generals to bring coups to salvage the critical situation in the country. Four army generals lead the army governments namely Field Marshall Mohammad Ayub Khan, General Yahya Khan, General Zia-ul Haq and General Pervez Musharraf; all of them were the heads of state during their tenure. The history tells us the legacy of Field Marshall Mohammad Ayub Khan who initiated the major economic reforms in Pakistan and strengthened the Pakistan Army which defeated India in 1965 war, the legacy of General Yahya Khan was to hold fair and free elections first time in the history of Pakistan, the legacy of General Zia-ul Haq was to accomplish successfully the nuclear power for Pakistan and to help Afghanis throw Russians out of Afghanistan, the legacy of General Pervez Musharraf was to bring stability and economic freedom to the country through major economic and social reforms and to gain respect for Pakistan and Pakistanis in the outside world. These generals later transpired themselves into some kind of democracy due to internal and external pressures i.e., Basic Democracy of General Mohammad Ayub Khan, Referendum and Non-party Elections of General Zia-ul Haq and the President Dominated Parliamentary System of General Pervez Musharraf. The periods ruled by at least two army generals i.e., General Mohammad Ayub Khan and General Pervez Musharraf is considered, by many, as the golden periods in the history of Pakistan during which Pakistan gained stability, economic freedom and foreign respect and the people of Pakistan made progress economically, socially and otherwise to enjoy a rather peaceful life.

What are the reasons for this reverse analogy in our country where the military regimes succeeded in giving good governance while the civilian regimes failed to provide leadership and good governance? The answer is very simple; the military regimes provided strong leadership and good governance free from major corruption and crimes. Pakistan ranked at the time when Pervez Musharraf took over the power as the world's 11th most corrupt nation but after Musharraf's government fought the corruption, Pakistan ranked in

2007 as the 41st most corrupt nation, a major improvement in a short period history also tells us that most of these military leaders were forced to leave the governments in the name of democracy; and what happened after their departure, the country once again went into the worst chaos and corruption and today the stability and safety of Pakistan is in serious danger.

What does this analysis mean to the people of Pakistan? Should the country be ruled by army in Pakistan? The answer is *No*. But what we should learn from these *stop-gap* governments of army generals or at least two of these army generals, the elements of their success behind their governance and that are (a) the strong and honest leadership; (b) the law and order in the country; (c) a fair and honest governance free from corruption, bribery, nepotism and injustices; (d) an honest and competent bureaucracy composed of capable and skilled people who can lead the country towards the prosperity and progress; and last but not least, (e) a tolerant society free from religious extremism, regional discrimination and linguistic preferences.

We have seen the 32 years of civilian governments and their consistent failures to govern which forced the army to rescue the situation in Pakistan. So, the question arises if the ruling party fails to govern and the safety of the country and its people becomes a serious issue, what other mechanism, if any, is available in the constitution of Pakistan to salvage the situation if the head of the state (generally appointed by the ruling party) refuses to take any action. Pakistan must find a solution to stop army coup in future and provide a mechanism in the constitution such as a Supreme Body comprised of heads of all major institutions in the country i.e., head of state, heads of government and the head of army who can force the ruling party to step down, if they fail to govern and the country goes in major chaos and call new elections. All corrupt politicians and bureaucrat responsible for such chaos must be barred from participating in future elections.

Today, Pakistan is being ruled by a democratically elected government of Asif Ali Zardari and Yousaf Raza Gillani of Pakistan Peoples Party, with their revolving alliances with other political parties, which obviously has failed, in my opinion, to provide the safety and security and good governance to its citizen. Pakistanis in a major turmoil; corruption is said to be at its highest level, leaders are known to be blindly robbing wealth from Pakistan, population seems to be on the verge of civil war and the safety of Pakistanis in serious danger. Foreign powers are conspiring to destabilize Pakistan and to destroy its nuclear strength. Where do we go from here? If the country survives till the next elections in 2013, can we expect a fair election by the corrupt ruling parties? Are we sure that the voters lists would not be tampered with? And above all, are we sure that the silent majority (60% population) of those who generally do not come out to vote in the elections would cross the barrier this time to defeat the current regime and its allies and help elect an honest leader and an honest party which can take the country out of current turmoil?

Pakistan is standing on a threshold, where Pakistan need a strong, credible and honest leadership; a leader who has a proven track record of providing strong leadership and who has demonstrated a good governance and who has the ability, honesty and the commitment to take Pakistan out of its current turmoil. Pakistan needs a leader who is respected by the Super powers of the world and who commands the respect and support from its own army and whose honesty, achievements and governance have been tested by the people of Pakistan People of Pakistan have already seen the present ruling party, its alliances and its official opposition (so hungry for power that they lost the touch of decent manner, calling President of Pakistan, the highest office in Pakistan by indecent names and slogans); electing any of these parties and their leaders, in my opinion, would be a grave mistake for Pakistan and for the people of Pakistan. Our people must realize by now that unless they all come out in large numbers (not conventional 40 to 45%) to defeat the current ruling parties, Pakistan's stability and safety will remain in danger and the people will still suffer from corruption. The voters in upcoming elections and specially those voters who conventionally did not vote in the past, must come out in great numbers to throw their strong support to a party and a leader who, they believe, can provide them with a strong leadership; who can bring law and order in the country; who can give a good governance and put an end to all corruption and injustices and bring immediate economic reforms to save hundreds and thousands of people who are struggling to barely survive.

Now the big question is, in today's horizon, who are those leaders and their parties who can find solutions to people's problems and can take the country out of current turmoil? The answer is simple, exclude all those parties and all those leaders who are already in power today and who are responsible to bring Pakistan near to being a failed state. This obviously brings ahead at least two known leaders who are currently campaigning for next elections and they are the former President of Pakistan and the head of All Pakistan Muslim League General Pervez Musharraf and the head of Tahrik-e-Insaf Imran Khan. Imran Khan, currently in forefront of politics, is no doubt an honest and dedicated leader, but in view of most political pundits, he seriously lacks the ability and leadership to govern a country that is in a major turmoil. Imran

Khan's leaning towards the extremist groups makes him unacceptable to major foreign powers of the world. On the other hand, General Pervez Musharraf who has launched his own political party All Pakistan Muslim League (APML) and is planning to go back to Pakistan to lead, what people believe, a revolution from Islamabad to Karachi, may be a right choice for Pakistan and the people of Pakistan. Pervez Musharraf is a strong and tested leader whose ability, honesty and leadership are known to the people of Pakistan. He maintains credible standing and strong leadership which is respected by major foreign powers of the world, a quality that no other leaders in Pakistan have today. Being a former army general he is respected by the army and carries their support to form the next government. His party is quickly gaining support from grassroots people and to my knowledge a significant number of elected or electable members of parliament have thrown their support behind him and are waiting for his arrival in Pakistan to launch an aggressive campaign for next elections. Musharraf, no doubt, has made a few political mistakes during his tenure, which he publicly admitted and apologized for, but he is not accused of any corruption and mismanagement and his tenure is termed by many as the golden era as compared to what they have seen in past three and a half years of the present regime.

Pakistanis in search of an honest and tested leader who can take the country out of its current unrest and misery and give the people of Pakistan hope for peaceful, happy and prosperous life. This can only happen if the voters show courage and willingness to fully participate, without any fear, in the next elections and not bow down against the corrupt and deceitful politicians who truly betrayed them in the past. Let me also say, if people do not come out to vote to elect a candidate and a party, they must certainly come out to vote against the corrupt and dishonest leaders and their parties to stop them from coming into power again. You can make the democracy work in Pakistan if all of you participate in the democratic process and participate in the elections. This is how a successful democracy works in other parts of the world.

God bless Pakistan and the people of Pakistan.

References

Published in The Lahore Times: November 1, 2011
Published in World News Network: November 1, 2011

ECP is discriminating against overseas Pakistanis

Pakistan must consider allocating a separate constituency and seats in the Pakistan national assembly for overseas Pakistanis

The recent directive issued by Mr. Ishtiaq Ahmad Khan, Secretary, Elections Commission of Pakistan (ECP), clearly shows his bias against the Pakistani citizens who are living abroad and hold the nationality of Pakistan.

The Friends of Pakistan in Canada strongly condemns Mr. Khan's directive and considers this as a discrimination against the Pakistani citizens, who live abroad; and are (1) equally loyal to Pakistan as those who live inside Pakistan; (2) full participants in the safety, security and well being of Pakistan and Pakistanis both outside and inside the country; and (3) contributing heavily in the well-being of Pakistan through remittances of over 14 billion dollars per year to Pakistan in foreign exchange and through other services.

The Friends of Pakistan in Canada is working on a "petition" to file in the Supreme Court of Pakistan as this declaration infringes the rights of Pakistanis living abroad. The Friends of Pakistan may also consider a class action against the EDC on behalf of overseas Pakistanis to protect their rights to take part in the elections in Pakistan.

There are millions of Pakistanis who live abroad and are very much part of Pakistan society similar to those who live inside Pakistan. The friends of Pakistan believe that constitution of Pakistan must acknowledge the residency status of these Pakistani as "overseas" and allocate a separate constituency and seats in the national assembly. The residency of Pakistani citizens does not conflict with their rights as a citizen since the residency of an individual depends on the economic, health, profession and other such factors.

The Friends of Pakistan believe that Mr. Khan is taking a narrow interpretation of both the Article 63(1) of the Constitution of Pakistan and

Section 99 (1A) (c) of the Representation of the People Act 1976 in view of the following arguments:

1. The spirit of the Article 63(1) and Section 99 (1A) (c) "... or acquire the citizenship of a foreign state" refers to those individuals who acquire the citizenship of a foreign state by giving up the citizenship of Pakistan. Pakistan can't take away the citizenship rights and privileges of an individual who remains as a Pakistani citizen (irrespective of the fact that the citizen lives outside Pakistan). A Pakistani citizen has a right to acquire an additional citizenship by virtue of living abroad as a "privilege" to avail additional benefits allowed under the laws of that foreign country.

2. The International Bill of Human Rights which consist of International Covenant of Civil and Political Rights (ICCPR) and Universal Declaration of Human Rights (UDHR) which states (a) "Everyone has the right to take part in the government of his/her country ..." Section 21(1) of ICCRP; (b) "Everyone has the right to a nationality" Article 15(1) of UDHR. The citizenship of a foreign country, which a Pakistani acquires without surrendering Pakistani citizenship, is considered as a "privilege" to enjoy the benefits of resident state but not as a "necessity" which can be acquired and also can be surrendered upon the free will of an individual.

3. It is a contradiction of the rights of a citizen who is allowed with all other rights as a citizen except taking part in the elections. The law cannot be prejudiced to bar any citizen from taking part in the election as long as he/she is a citizen of Pakistan.

4. The definition of Article 63(1) and Section 99 (1A) (c) to include an overseas Pakistani as a citizen eligible to take part in the elections can be interpreted by the courts under the "Doctrine of State Necessity" as the residency of a Pakistani in overseas is positively contributing to the safety, security and the well-being of Pakistan and the citizens of Pakistan.

5. There are other countries of the world including Canada that allow an individual with dual nationality to take part in their elections.

The Friends of Pakistan firmly believes that overseas Pakistanis are very much part of the Pakistani society and they should not be deprived of any political or social rights as granted under the constitution to the citizens of Pakistan.

At the end, we believe that excluding overseas Pakistanis from a political process will cause serious damages to Pakistan and the people of Pakistan as everyone who lives abroad is an ambassador and well-wisher of Pakistan and the dual nationality is simply a privilege which they acquire to gain benefits while they are resident of a foreign country.

References

Published in The Lahore times: December 21, 2011
Published in World News Network: December 22, 2011

Next general election is a test of people's power in Pakistan

It's a time for 60% non-participating voters to join 40% conventional voters to elect a leader who can salvage the situation in Pakistan

Voters must look at the history of politicians and their political parties before they cast their ballots in next elections

General (Retd) Pervez Musharraf is the only viable option to take Pakistan out of current crises based on his leadership skills and past performance

On October 30, 1995 when a ruling party of the province of Quebec in Canada called a referendum and tried to separate Quebec from Canada by seeking independence; 94% of all eligible voters in the province of Quebec came out and the majority of them voted "NO" against the separation. Do you know why? Because the voters realized that the time had come to show their "power" to safeguard the unity of their land. Today, the separatist movement is almost dead and the people of Quebec are enjoying the fruits of united Canada. This is how the power of people works under a democratic system.

Pakistan is in a major turmoil today; the corruption, lawlessness and the poverty in the country are at their peak; people's lives and their properties and investments are not safe; violence and terrorism have gone beyond the control of government, foreign intervention and aggression across the borders of Pakistan have grown to new heights, confrontation between the government and its establishment has reached to an alarming limit, the conspiracy and scandal against the state are very much in the air and the tussle between the supreme court and the government seems to be not going away. The war of words between the ruling party and the opposition has gone from a normal civilized limit to highly uncivilized limits. In other words, the country is in major catastrophic state and its institutions seem to be on the brink of disaster and bankruptcy.

Ali Abbas Hasanie and Pervez Musharraf in a Fund Raising Dinner in Montreal, Canada Photo courtesy of APML Montreal Chapter

The question now arises how the "power of people" can save Pakistan from this turmoil? The answer is simple; by defeating the ruling parties and their official opposition in the polls and by electing leaders who are honest and who have proven records of strong leadership, administrative skills and political wisdom to understand and find solutions for difficult issues faced by the nation. The champions of democratic system have identified three key components which make a democratic system work i.e., (1) the Voters, (2) the Elections and (3) the Leaders and their political parties. The 2013 elections are around the corner in Pakistan and the voters need to understand the importance, implications and the application of these key components before they support any leader and/or decide to votes for any political party.

The first key element is the "Voters" namely the "People of Pakistan". Voters no doubt have the absolute "Power" to elect the "Rulers of State" in the elections but they are faced with many challenges such as (1) lower turn-out of voters on the polling day; (2) voting behavior of people based on loyalties; (3) dishonesty, deception, and manipulation of facts by the leaders and their party candidates; and last but not least (4) the voting irregularities i.e., the corruption, rigging, fraud, intimidation and the state intervention.

The question arises how can a voter fight and overcome these challenges? The answer is by gaining "awareness" of the issues confronting Pakistan and the people of Pakistan; and by raising themselves above all "loyalties" (except the loyalty to state). Once Quaid-e-Azam, the founder of Pakistan, gave this message to the nation: ". . . come forward and rise to the occasion. You have performed wonder in the past. . . . you are not lacking in the great qualities and virtues . . . only you have to be fully conscious of the fact and to act with courage, faith and unity".

Unlike countries such as Belgium, Australia, Brazil, Turkey and others, it is not mandatory to cast your ballots in general elections in Pakistan; as a result the history of voters turnout in Pakistan between 1988 to 2008 shows that on average only 42.2% of registered voters or 38.9 % of total eligible voters voted in the past seven elections.

The absence of about 60% voters from the voting process is a major set back to the democratic process and the "power of the people" in Pakistan. We all know when the question of breaking the country came in Canada in 1995, 94% all eligible voters turned out voluntarily and defeated the option of Quebec separation. Today, Pakistan is in a major turmoil and its security is on stake; it is a time for the 60% voters, who historically did not participate in voting, to join the 40% conventional voters to defeat corrupt leaders and to elect a leader who can salvage the situation in Pakistan.

Let us now look at voters behavior; it is true that the voters in Pakistan come from different backgrounds and regions and with different priorities and loyalties but one thing common in all voters is that they all "love" Pakistan and they all are ready to "fight" to save the destruction of Pakistan. The people of Pakistan must put the interest of Pakistan first and has to raise themselves above all loyalties by breaking the barriers which divide them in the elections such as regional segregation (provincial, or rural and urban considerations); linguistic distinctions (Punjabi, Sindhi, Urdu, Balouchi, Pashto); *biradari* system (Syed, Sheikh, Jatt, Rajput, Arain, Kharel, Balouch, Pashtun, etc.); and the religious, cast and creed preferences (Sunni, Shia, Wahhabi, Devbandi, Barailwi, etc.).

The history of general elections in Pakistan is unfortunately very bleak. There were no direct elections at the national level between 1947 and 1969. With the exception of elections held under the army in 1970, all other national elections from 1977 to 2008, according to independent observers, were not fair and created a culture of rigging, fraud, intimidation and the state patronage. People must reject this culture by taking a much stronger stand against the irregularities in elections; a stand such as the people of Pakistan had taken after the rigging of 1977 elections. Today, some of the political leaders and their parties are demanding to involve the army and the judiciary in the administration of upcoming national elections. Looking at the results of past elections, this demand seems to be reasonable and can be implemented if the Supreme Court of Pakistan at its own cognizance through *suo motu* orders the interim government to involve the institutions of justice and the army to ensure free and fair elections. It is widely believed that the Supreme Court of Pakistan can play a very major role in this difficult time in Pakistan, because people of Pakistan have full confidence in Justice Iftikhar Muhammad Chaudhry and his panel of judges to deliver absolute "justice" whether it be elections administration or "Memogate" or "Benazir's murder" or any other cases before supreme court especially relating to politicians.

The manipulation of facts and misstatements, during the elections, is a common phenomenon in Pakistan by the leaders and their political parties; but dishonesty, deception and fraud with the voters through "straight lies" and "fraudulent statements" by denying facts and deliberately misquoting information are not a common culture in the elections of a civilized society. While it is upon voters to verify the facts and identify the leaders who lie and whose statements are not credible, the public media also bears the responsibility to play an impartial role to uncover the leaders' lies and frauds to the voters since they are equipped with the information and documents in their libraries to support the truth. For example, there is a leader and a party head in Pakistan who is portraying himself as an honest and credible leader these days but there are legal documents and a documentary film uncovering his frauds, crimes and money laundering which has already been made public and shown on television in the past and are still available in the records and archives.

There are seven major political parties which held seats in the national assembly of Pakistan between 1970 and 2008 namely (1) Pakistan People's Party (PPP), (2) Pakistan Muslim League—Nawaz Group (PML-N), (3) Pakistan Muslim League—Quaid-e-Azam (PML-Q) (4) Muttahida Qaumi Movement (MQM), (5) Awami National Party (ANP), (6) Pakistan Muslim League—Functional (PML-F) and (7) Muttahida Majlis-e-Amal Pakistan, conglomeration of Islamic parties (MMAP). There are two other political parties who are not in the parliament but their leaders are well known and they are on forefront of today's politics i.e., Pakistan Tahreek-e-Insaf-Imran

Khan (PTI) and All Pakistan Muslim League—General (Retd.) Pervez Musharraf (APML).

Pakistan People's Party (PPP)—Zulfiqar Ali Bhutto, after resigning from the government of Ayub Khan, founded PPP in 1967 initially to take revenge from his old boss Ayub Khan, on so called humiliation suffered by Pakistan at the negotiation table of Tashkent. PPP has formed the government four times since its first controversial victory in 1970; their government under Zulfiqar Ali Bhutto was dissolved by the army due to major chaos caused by the rigging of 1977 elections; its governments under Begum Benazir Bhutto in 1988 and 1993 were sacked both times by the President on the charges of corruption, lawlessness and misuse of power. The current government under President Asif Ali Zardari and Prime Minister Yousuf Raza Gilani, elected in 2008, is blamed to bring the country to a major turmoil and the brink of bankruptcy due to alleged corruption, mismanagement and lawlessness. On the other hand, the overturn of NRO by the Supreme Court has once again brought back the court cases of fraud and money laundering against the President, and the alleged PPP role in recent Memogate scandal, which is causing havoc in the country.

Pakistan Muslim League—Nawaz (PML-N)—Mian Mohammad Nawaz Shariff of Pakistan Muslim League—Nawaz (PML-N) joined politics in 1970 after his family owned business was nationalized by PPP. Nawaz Shariff formed the government two times; the first time in 1990 after joining the coalition of Islami Jamhoori Ittihad created by General Zia-ul Haq, his government was sacked by the President on the charges of corruption and misuse of power; his second time government in 1997, after he declared his own PML-N, was dissolved by the army on the charges of corruption, money laundering and plane hijacking to create terror and insecurity for the people on board including army chief. Nawaz Shariff was charged, convicted and imprisoned for life in the hijacking case but on the request of a friendly foreign government, his life imprisonment was replaced by an exile to Saudi Arabia upon signing of an agreement between him, his family and the government. The President, in a "plea bargain", pardoned the corruption cases and sentences against him on the grounds that he was leaving on exile.

PML-Q was established in 2001 as a result of major defection from PML-N of senior politicians. PML-Q formed the government in 2002, which completed its five year term. General Pervez Musharraf who was the President spearheaded the government, which according to international sources, positively contributed to the well being of people and in the progress of the country economically, socially and politically. The corruptions created during the previous regimes were brought down to 41st most corrupt nation from 11th most corrupt nation in the world. Also, Pakistan was graded amongst the 11 most developing countries in the world at that time. General Pervez Musharraf promoted a moderate, enlightened and progressive democracy with wisdom, tolerance and social justice; free from religious extremism and regional discrimination. The opponents in three major issues i.e., Lal Masjid, Akbar Bugti and NRO, however, are accusing General Pervez Musharraf. While Pervez Musharraf explained the circumstances and the background of NRO, he maintains that the Lal Masjid and Akbar Bugti actions were the result of normal administrative measures of the state under the circumstances, which his opponents are exploiting to gain political mileage. PML-Q is reduced substantially due to defection of his key party members on the ground that hierarchy of the party is being involved in so called corruption.

MQM, MMAP and ANP have never formed the government but were either in alliance or opposition of the governing parties. Although MQM and ANP have strong holds in their home ridings their chances of gaining majority in the parliament and forming a government are highly unlikely. These parties at times held the balance of power in parliament and became important partners in forming a coalition government. MMAP presently is dysfunctional and only one faction Jamiat-Ulma-e-Islam of Maulana Fazl-ur Rehman has gained a few seats in 2008 elections, again all in the province of Khyber Pakhtunkhwa.

Pakistan Tahreek-e-Insaf (PTI) was established in 1996 by Imran Khan but hardly gained any seat in the national assembly except for Imran Khan in 2002. Imran Khan, the leader of PTI is a successful cricketer, a cricket commentator and philanthropist but has never been exposed to any administrative role in the government or to a leadership of a party that formed the government in the country. In the midst of major controversies against PPP and PML-N, Imran Khan and his party PTI is emerging on the political scene as a third political force. But the current influx of old politicians, tainted with what some observers believe the corruption and failed managements, from PPP, PML-N and PML-Q to his party is damaging the image of PTI whose leader is known as an honest man not involved in any corruption. The inclusion of old politicians according to some analysts may be politically strengthening the party position in elections but the political pundits are seriously questioning if PTI is becoming a party of recycled politicians who ruled the country in the past supporting dishonest and corrupt leaderships. Imran Khan as a party leader is an honest individual but his lack of wisdom towards a faction in Afghan war and towards the war against terrorism is very much obvious from his policy statements. The political observers are also questioning his lack of experience in leadership to deal with extremely difficult situation faced by Pakistan and its national institutions.

General (Retd.) Pervez Musharraf, who is fluent in politics and well-versed with military tactics comes from an army background similar to some prominent political leaders of the world such as Winston Churchill (Officer in British Army), Charles de Gaulle (Army General in French Forces in World War II) and Dwight David Eisenhower (Five Star General in the US Army and Commander of Allied Forces in Europe in World War II) and George Washington (Commander-in-Chief of the Continental Army). General (Retd.) Pervez Musharraf founded APML in August 2010 and launched his party in October 2010 as a political movement that is committed to bring about the political reforms in Pakistan. General Pervez Musharraf, governed Pakistan from October 1999 till August 2008 and according to independent political observers the Musharraf years yielded significant dividends to Pakistan such as his economic and social achievements for the well-being of Pakistan and the people of Pakistan, his commitment to tackle terrorism, his ability to promote dialogue with Indian government, especially over Kashmir, and above all his actions to root out corruption in the country. The foreign governments have great respect for his honesty and leadership and praised him as one of the world's most committed partners in the war against terrorism and extremism and claim that the world had no fear about the nuclear proliferation during his time. Sattar Edhi, a well-known social and humanitarian worker, praised Pervez Musharraf as an honest and dedicated leader and wished he could have remained in power for the prosperity and well being of the people of Pakistan. Pervez Musharraf has announced to go back to Pakistan by the end of this month, to actively campaign for the upcoming elections and to build the party structure to meet the challenges faced to Pakistan and the people of Pakistan.

Pakistan as a nation is a member of the community of nations in the world and carries global responsibly to maintain peace and harmony by working with other nations to provide security and safety to his citizens as well as to the citizens of other countries. Pakistan is also a member of nuclear family that puts an added responsibility on Pakistan to assure that their nuclear materials are secure and the world should not worry about nuclear proliferation and its misuse. Therefore, the leaders of Pakistan have responsibility to avoid unnecessary confrontation and criticism against the world powers in order to gain political mileage for their party in the upcoming elections. Pakistan has built good relationship with the world powers during Pervez Musharraf period by joining hands to fight against terrorism and extremism and any attempt to label this as "a war of a third nation" would simply deteriorate our relationship with countries who are helping Pakistan in its national security and economical well being.

The current uprising and the "political awareness" in Pakistan clearly demonstrate that the days of feudal lords and corrupt politicians are numbered and the people of Pakistan are getting ready to use their "voting power" to elect a party and a leader who is honest and capable and who can stand with them shoulder to shoulder to fight for the security, well being and the prosperity of Pakistan and the people of Pakistan. The overwhelming crowds and enthusiasm in non-ruling party *jalsas* is a sign that people want a "change" in government. Based on above analyses, it goes without saying that, in my opinion, the people of Pakistan have only two choices i.e., Imran Khan (PTI) or Pervez Musharraf (APML) who are honest, trustworthy and free from allegations of corruption, nepotism and money laundering. The political opponents of these leaders are becoming desperate and more vocal by fabricating "truth", spreading "lies" and creating "conspiracies" against Imran and Musharraf. But they know, the people of Pakistan are ready to vote out all old political parties and their leaders and are ready to vote for a leader who is capable of dealing with "transparency in government", "elimination of corruption", "economic growth", "employment opportunities", "elimination of terrorism and extremism", "transparency in judicial system" and of course "good relations with other nations including India".

I have already discussed in detail the history of voters, elections and leaders and their parties in my analyses, I am sure that the people of Pakistan know the issues confronting Pakistan and the people of Pakistan and they are certainly ready to use the "People's Power" to save Pakistan by bringing an honest, capable and tested leader and his party who can deal with the current turmoil, crush corruption and bring the rule of law, restore economic prosperity and eliminate poverty, fight terrorism and extremism and bring the peace and harmony in the society, eliminate confrontation and create ideal relations with major powers of the world and above all give justice, peace and happiness to the people of Pakistan. The impartial political observers both in Pakistan and other part of the world are of the opinion that General (Retd.) Pervez Musharraf is the only viable option under the circumstances to take Pakistan out of current crises based on his leadership skills and past performances.

Pakistan Zindabad.

References

Published in The Lahore Times: January 16, 2012
Published in World News Network: January 17, 2012

Pakistan must adopt a National Unity Bill in parliament

Pakistan must consider adopting a national unity bill in parliament to bury old hatchets and kill political scandals to create normal environment conducive for elections and the governance after elections

National security of Pakistan is at risk if politicians continue to attack on the name of democracy the very institutions responsible for peace, security and justice in the country

National security of Pakistan is at risk if politicians continue to attack Pakistan's two most respected institutions; namely the Army and the Judiciary in the name of democracy. The current situation of confrontation between politicians and the army and judiciary is causing major concerns amongst the people of Pakistan who depend on these institutions to bring peace, security and justice in a country which is hit by worst corruption, highest unemployment, unforeseen hikes in prices and the acute shortage of power, gas and items of vital survival for the people of Pakistan.

Pakistan is faced with unprecedented political scandals and controversies, which may turn into a great national tragedy if the establishment and institutions do not come to a common platform to resolve these issues constitutionally and politically. It is a time of national reconciliation to safeguard the national security and rescue democracy, the democracy which, in the opinion of many observers, has not contributed to the well being of Pakistan and the people of Pakistan in the last four years of an elected government.

Today, the national security of Pakistan is in serious danger on the face of growing controversies on (1) Memogate scandal, (2) Air Marshal Asghar Khan's petition, (3) contempt of the Supreme Court against prime minister Yousaf Raza Gilani, (4) impeachment attempts against President Asif Ali Zardari and the former President General (Retd.) Pervez Musharraf, (5) revival of cases against NRO culprits, and above all (6) the suspension of membership of 28 members of national parliament and provincial assemblies by the Supreme Court causing major constitutional and legal consequences as the parliament is failing to passage the 20th Constitutional Amendment in the horse trading between ruling parties and the opposition.

Memogate—if parties involved are proven guilty in the court, Pakistan's former US ambassador, the President of Pakistan and possibly more people could end up with treason charges and impeachment, a situation which will further infuriate the crises in the country as the army and the Supreme Court may hound the current civilian government to resign.

Air Marshal (Retd.) Asghar Khan's petition—if the cases of bribery through ISI which acted on the instructions of a former President of Pakistan and the army chief, are proven in the court and punished, it will take Pakistan's politics into an uncharted territory by holding to account under civilian laws the military's ISI directorate. Also, the alleged recipients of so called bribery, which includes the names of heads of leading political parties in today's politics and prominent politicians, if get convicted and punished, or legally barred by the Supreme Court to take part in the elections under article 63 of the constitution will further contribute to an already major turmoil in the country.

The contempt of the Supreme Court against the Prime Minister—the sentencing by the SC of Prime Minister Yousuf Raza Gilani on February 13, 2012, may send him to jail and also bar him from taking part in future elections. The extinction of Yousuf Raza Gilani's political carrier to save the President of Pakistan and other high-profile accused of famous NRO, in the opinion of most observers, may bring strong public reaction, similar to what we have seen in Musharraf's days, as the supporters of PPP believe that the elected government of PPP and their allied parties is being hurdled by "governments within government" to fail the democratically elected government.

November 2007 Emergency Ordinance—if former President Pervez Musharraf ends up with treason charges on this issue, his attorneys will certainly drag into this treason case other army generals, officers and leaders who participated in imposing of the state of emergency as well as the Supreme Court judges who validated the 2007 Emergency Ordinance. The institutions of Army and Judiciary, in view of most observers, would certainly not like to see their former chief and associates being impeached and perhaps punished

31

for an act, which some observers believe, were quite within the constitutional power of the President. The ruling party may also lose its alliance if the leaders of allied parties are victimized in this case. This will open a new front and will cause a major chaos in the country.

The revival of cases dropped under NRO deal—originally brokered by the United States, consisting of 8,041 accused, if pursued in the Supreme Court may bring serious ramifications and perhaps guilty verdicts of fines and punishments against a number of prominent leaders from ruling and opposition parties and their allies, including the President of Pakistan and few current and former government ministers and parliamentarians. It is interesting to note here that the government was given 120 days on December 16, 2009 by the Supreme Court to regularize the NRO through the parliament, which the government failed to comply. If the Supreme Court now awards guilty verdicts against accused, they may be disqualified under Article 63 of the constitution to take part in upcoming elections. This will throw the country into major political crises and probably the supporters of barred politicians may stages protests, rallies, *dharnas* and strikes, which will further destabilize the situation in Pakistan. Moreover, the political parties (encouraged by the court's decisions) may jam the Supreme Court by filing more corruption charges against each other which will create an environment of controversies and unrest in the country.

Apart from the above cases, the recent suspension of members of national and provincial assemblies along with the suspension of future elections and by-elections due to the, so-called, deficient Election Commission, incomplete and bogus electoral list and the ineligibility of MPs with fake degrees as well as those who got elected with bogus voters lists are some major issues that touch the nerves of most of the leading political parties; and a timely resolution of these issues before the elections seems difficult if not impossible. The Supreme Court has pointed out some of these issues to attorney general on May 9, 2011, and given the government time to rectify this anomaly but the government failed to pass required amendment through the parliament. At the time of writing this article, the government has not yet reached a consensus with the opposition on the contents of the amendment of Bill 20 and PML-N is playing hardball with PPP to include those items in this bill which are not an immediate concern of the court. The expulsion of elected members and failure to reach a resolution to the satisfaction of the people of Pakistan may ignite a political situation in which a large number of students, lawyers and political supporters may come out on the streets to protest against fallen MPs and the cancellation of elections, to what we have seen after the 1977 elections.

The analyses of these political scandals and controversies suggests that Pakistan has become a battlefield for the so-called power play between government, army, judiciary and politicians; apparently with no respect to Pakistan or the national security of Pakistan and no respect for the people or well-being of the people of Pakistan. The government of the day believes that they hold supreme power in the country to do every right or wrong because they are elected by the people of Pakistan. The history, however, tells us that between 1970 and 2012, out of eight elected governments that came into power, only three of them completed their full 5-year terms (including the current PPP government); five elected government were dissolved by the heads of state or the army in turmoil caused by corruption, lawlessness and misuse of power.

The institution of armed forces, which constitutionally comes under the President, bears the responsibility of national security of Pakistan and the protection and administration of nuclear warheads. However, when there is a major turmoil in the country, the people and sometimes politicians look upon the army as a savior to bring peace, security and also economic well being to the people. Although the army should never derail the democracy in the country, there came a time when the security of Pakistan became an issue which allowed army to bring coups d'état in Pakistan at four different occasions, all of them were initially welcome by the general public and even some politicians and were approved by the Supreme Court of Pakistan. General Ashfaq Parvez Kayani, the Army Chief, has made a statement that army has no desire to derail democracy; but most of the observers believe that, God forbid, if the time comes the Pakistan army cannot sit idle and watch the destruction of Pakistan through internal and external forces all in the name of supporting democracy.

**Ali Abbas Hasanie—in a Montreal Community Meeting Photo
courtesy of Weekly Ummeed, Newspaper Canada**

Although the institution of judiciary comes under the government, the constitution gives it complete independence to exercise justice and ensure law and order in the country. Conventionally judiciary exercises self-restraint since it is appointed by the administration but is not directly accountable to the people. The followers of judicial activism, however, justify the role of judiciary going beyond self-restraint to exercise judicial activism through *suo motu* on the grounds that it is vital to ensure a "Just" and "Stable" society which is a big question mark in the country these days. Unfortunately, when the justice takes its course in cases related to executive branch of government or the politicians, then the incidents such as the attack on the Supreme Court by Nawaz Sharif's supporters or contempt of court act by Yousuf Raza Gilani occur.

The root cause of almost all of the above scandals and controversies goes back to our politicians; and today the situation in the country has reached to such a point where foreign observers and press are labeling Pakistan as a failed state. Often the former President of Pakistan general (Retd.) Pervez Musharraf, who is respected by foreign press, comes on their podium and press and defends Pakistan as a democratic and progressive country with nuclear capability to defend against any foreign aggression. In the midst of such a critical situation in Pakistan, our politicians or political parties are exploiting the situation to take an advantage in the elections by slinging mud on each other to create more sensation in an already torn environment. While the members of most of the political parties are involved in above scandals, one way or the other they are all playing games with the national security without much respect to the integrity of Pakistan and the fragile situation of the people of Pakistan. The media is pre-occupied with these scandals and there is hardly any time available on media to look at other critical issues faced to Pakistan on global scenes and to talk about the peace, prosperity and well-being of the people of Pakistan.

Pakistan is in a major state of turmoil; its national security is seriously in danger and the people of Pakistan are struggling to see a meaningful change in the country. The current shifts to political parties support will give rise to polarization between parties directly identifying themselves to Islamic *'ittehad'* (alliance) against other political parties that are constantly back biting each other by rejecting *ittehad*. This will drag people's focus from issues critical to the survival of Pakistan to non-issues, which will be dividing the population of Pakistan. The debate over issues inflaming regional feelings to attract votes by the politicians may escalate tensions over the regional disparities and incidents, which may support the cause of external powers to diminish the geo-political strength of Pakistan to support their desire to disintegrate Pakistan thereby fulfilling their dreams of "obtaining access" to warm waters and the creation of a war territory on the borders of Iran. Often conspired by external powers, the constant unrest and change of power in Muslim worlds, ranging from Sudan, Tunis, Yemen, Iraq, Afghanistan, Egypt, Libya, Bahrain and now Syria, seems to be approaching to Iran and therefore Pakistan should not consider itself exempt from these anti-Muslim movements. The recent support of Russia and China to defeat the resolution in the Security Council against Syria is another reason to escalate the trouble in regions where Russia and China are involved.

It is high time to put politics on aside and come to a common platform to reconcile differences and bring "national unity" in Pakistan. Political leaders must fully understand that their urge to capture the "power" does not prevail over the security of Pakistan. The current turmoil in the country in which serious confrontation exists between the government, army, Supreme Court and the political parties is a time of "reconciliation for national unity" not the elections or the power-play for elections. The political scholars and senior observers believe that the current turmoil can only be resolved by a "negotiated solution" in which all parties involved in confrontation must agree to present and pass a "National Unity Bill" in the parliament which will allow the President to grant full, free and absolute pardon to all parties involved in scandals and court cases and pave the way to a peaceful environment which is needed for the elections and most importantly after the elections for ruling party to have all-party cooperation to govern the country.

The proposed National Unity Bill to be presented in the parliament, must include all scandals and controversies ranging from Memogate to the threat to President and former President for treason charges and impeachment and must be acceptable to the Supreme Court of Pakistan, who in the opinion of most observers, is looking for a mutual resolution of all issues without jeopardizing the constitution. This National Unity Bill will allow politicians to bury all old hatchets and kill all political scandals and controversies to help create a conducive environment for upcoming general elections and after the elections for the governance of elected government to work in the best interest of Pakistan and the people of Pakistan.

The history tells us that in a somewhat similar turmoil in the USA in 1974, Gerald R. Ford, the President of United States granted a full, free and absolute pardon unto Richard Nixon, the former President of the USA for all his offences against the state. Because the prospects of impeachment trial could have caused a prolonged and divisive debate over the propriety of exposing further issues which would have grown from a political scandal into a national tragedy.

Let us join hands to unite ourselves and show patriotism, tolerance and love for Pakistan and the people of Pakistan.

PAKISTAN ZINDABAD

References

Published in The Lahore Times: February 13, 2012

Pakistan a democratic country without an official opposition in parliament

Pakistan is a democratic country without an official opposition in parliament to stop the government from unconstitutional, unethical and inhuman deeds

Doctrine of "Mukh Mukha" (give and take) is being pursued by corrupt politicians to use the act of "Bandar Baat" (unjust sharing) between political parties in parliament

Parliamentary majority is being misused to defy the constitution and to subvert the democratic process to retain power in the face of worst crisis in Pakistan

Government is defying the orders of supreme court and refusing to accept its supremacy which may lead to the prospect of SC exercising its power to control the law & order situation and to call immediate general elections

On June 8-10, 1998 in London, England, a workshop on the "rights and responsibilities of the Opposition" was organized by the Commonwealth Secretariat and the Commonwealth Parliamentary Association which was also attended by Barrister Chaudhry Aitzaz Ahsan, former Minister of Law and Justice in Pakistan in the Benazir Bhutto's government. The conference concluded that an effective and responsible opposition is essential for the success of parliamentary democracy; and it is vital to maintain a clear distinction between the roles of the Opposition and the Government, especially to ensure that the independence of the former was not compromised. In other words, where it is essential for a democratically elected government to serve the best interest of the people of the country; the official Opposition is equally essential to be in touch with and to understand and defend the needs and the interests of the people who elected them.

On March 31, 2008 Pakistan's People Party (PPP) won most seats in the parliament; however, their numbers were short to form a majority government. Therefore, they formed a coalition government with the alliance of Pakistan Muslim League—Nawaz group (PML-N) the second largest seat holders in the parliament and Awami National Party (ANP) by consolidating their collective voting power to 67% (or over 2/3 majority) in the parliament. It was obvious that this alliance was created not to give good governance to the people of Pakistan but to settle the account with President General Pervez Musharraf, in whose eight years of rule, the heads of at least two major political parties in this alliance were charged with (and in one case convicted of) corruption, misuse of power and criminal acts. PPP made alliances in the parliament initially with PML-N and ANP and later with PML-Q, MQM and JUI (after PML-N pulled out of the alliance) in order to form a coalition government with the obvious mission to stabilize the democracy and out-perform the government of the so called dictator General Pervez Musharraf who, in the opinion of most observers, provided a relatively stable government with notable economic success and significant social reforms in the country.

PML-N, which won the second largest number of seats in the national assembly, decided to abdicate the role of official Opposition, usually assumed by the party having the second largest number of seats in the parliament. They joined the ruling party, what is largely believed, in their self-interests to remove President General Musharraf and to undo the acts implemented during Musharraf regime. The alliance of ruling PPP with other parties to form a majority government, gave a clear signal to the public that the government holds an absolute power in the parliament to govern without a fear of no-confidence against any of their failed or fouled policies, all in the name of democracy, to serve the interests of allied political partners with no respect for the needs and the interest of the people who elected them. The PML-N's departure from parliamentary alliance was not meant to allow it to sit in the parliament as an official Opposition but to go somewhere in a buffer zone to hold a sword on the head of PPP on issues which can serve their political interest and not the interests of general public who elected them.

Today, after four and half years in power of these democratically elected parties in parliament, Pakistan is facing the worst crisis in the history of Pakistan. The corruption has hit an all time high record in 64 years of history of Pakistan, poverty and unemployment have broken all previous records, basic needs of people such as electricity, gas and food items are either not available or available at prices beyond the reach of an average person and the law and order situation in the country is so bad that it is becoming hard to safeguard lives, properties, businesses and worship places. The country has been drowned in national debt in last four and half years which is much more than the collective debts of last 60 years; and the national institutions are on the verge of collapsing. Supreme Court is overloaded with cases of corruption, lawlessness and inhuman treatment of citizens. Cities are faced with worst killings and unrest and the people are being robbed in broad daylight. To add insult to injury the recent flagrant refusal of Prime Minister to accept the decision of Supreme Court has opened a new front in already severe constitutional and political crises in the country. People of Pakistan are questioning, where is the official Opposition in parliament to raise the concerns of the common man and to stop the government from further complicating the law and order situation in the country.

While people are up in arms and crying for help, the major political parties in the parliament are all occupied with their own political agendas and their leaders under the doctrine of *"Mukh Mukha—MM"* (Give and Take) are involved in the act of *"Bandar Baat—BB"* (Unjust sharing) with no respect for the problems and needs of people. Their first major achievement under the doctrine of MM was to remove General Pervez Musharraf from the Presidency and to bring the 18th amendment to strengthen the hands of parliament to facilitate the so-called act of BB in the absence of Official Opposition. Their next achievement was to defy the orders of Supreme Court and undermine the strength of the establishment to provide escape for NRO culprits and to cause incidents such as Memogate scandal against the establishment. The political partners of PPP under the doctrine of MM are all silent as they know that one day they will need the reciprocal support from PPP when the Asghar Khan Petition case reaches the final verdict stage before the SC and the implementation of 20th amendment comes to play at the time of elections.

In my article "Pakistan a nation in search of a leader", I questioned the process of democracy in Pakistan where 60% impartial and fair minded people do not participate in the voting process and biased and socially pressured voters take up the polls to cast fair and unfair votes to the party and candidates of their choices. Consequently, the political parties and their leaders elected under these circumstances do not feel obligated to serve the entire population but to serve the interests of those handful of people who manipulated the system to bring them into power. In another article "Next general election is a test of people's power in Pakistan", I appealed to the 60% non-participating voters to come out and salvage the situation in Pakistan. The history of corrupt politicians and their parties is not hidden from anyone in Pakistan (read my article) and it is a time for the people of Pakistan to use "People Power" and save Pakistan.

The prerequisites of any democratic system are (1) strong and well-respected national institutions such as the judiciary, armed forces, education, health, human rights, elections commission and above all the government of the day; (2) strong, capable, honest and respected leadership; (3) impartial and unbiased media; and (4) the most important the "Voters" who must not compromise their votes under any social pressures, monetary gains and/or regional and linguistic barriers.

The demographic composition in Pakistan today gives a clear lead (53% +) to young generation between the ages of 18-35 years whose approach towards the democracy in Pakistan is drastically different from their elders; they like honest and capable leaders vs. corrupt and failed leaders; they reject regional, linguistic and sectarian distinctions in the society and they hate social pressures, bribes and undue influences in elections; they truly believe in "just society" and "equality" for all irrespective of race, colour, religion and other disparities. This crowd is actively taking part in political rallies and often seen in great numbers in Imran Khan's political meetings; a clear indication for a change in government in Pakistan.

As ruling parties are reaching the end of their current mandate, their strategies also include stopping the upcoming political forces of those honest and credible leaders who may become a challenge for them in the next general elections. It is very obvious to the people of Pakistan that the current ruling parties in the parliament have miserably failed and the people are looking for a "change" to elect honest and capable leaders and their parties who can take the country out of the current turmoil.

Ali Abbas Hasanie addressing the audience on Pakistan Resolution Day in Montreal Canada Photo courtesy of Pakistan Association of Quebec, Montreal

Imran Khan of PTI and General Pervez Musharraf of APML, in the opinion of most political observers, are two prominent leaders in Pakistan who are honest and capable and the people will no doubt elect them in the next general elections if the parliamentary majority is not used to subvert the democratic process. The passing of the 20th Amendment in the constitution which allows PPP and PML-N (without consultation with other prominent political parties such as PTI and APML) to form a partial interim government and the Elections Commission to conduct the elections with a questionable voters lists; threatening of General Pervez Musharraf with impeachment under Article 6 if he comes back to Pakistan to participate in the political process which may cause an alliance with Imran Khan to strengthen the power of honest and credible leaders; and to defy the orders of SC which may open a can of worms on the corruption of leaders whose parties are in the parliament, are few examples of the acts under the doctrine of MM which can be paralleled with the misuse of parliamentary power to tamper with the democratic process.

The political observers, independent media and the main opposition parties outside the parliament are all demanding that the government must respect the court orders and the supremacy of Supreme Court and call free and fair elections under an impartial interim government and the Elections Commission with a legitimate voters list approved by all parties; failing which the country may fall into a major chaos unprecedented to what the people of Pakistan have seen on the streets after the 1977 elections or for the restoration of CJ and supreme court judges in the past. If the situation further deteriorates and the security of the country and the people of Pakistan is further jeopardized, the political scholars and the jurists are predicting that Supreme Court of Pakistan will exercise its powers under the constitution to control the law and order situation and to call an immediate general election by installing an impartial interim government which may include retired judges of supreme court and the members of armed forces of Pakistan.

References

Published in The Lahore Times: May 2, 2012

President must dissolve parliament immediately to appoint a caretaker government

President must dissolve parliament immediately to appoint a caretaker government to avoid further deterioration and anarchy in Pakistan

Three months conventional period may not be enough for interim government to normalize conditions before next general elections

ON FEBRUARY 18, 2013 the current parliament will complete its five years term, however, the growing confrontation between the government and the judiciary as well as the defiance by national institutions to abide by government directives, are making both government and the parliament a lame duck to run the affairs of the state. The anarchy in the country has reached to such a height that major cities such as Karachi, Lahore and Quetta have become non-functional and people in these cities are hiding inside their homes to take refuge from target killings, *bhatta khori* (ransom), abduction and such other horrible crimes. Businesses are completely shutting down and necessities of life are becoming hard to get by ordinary citizens in Pakistan.

The question then arises why the governing parties and so-called friendly apposition in the parliament are not serious to stop further deterioration and anarchy and call general elections? The answer is simple, PPP and their allies are still negotiating with PML-N (friendly opponents) and others on seat adjustments in next elections; and they want to maintain 2/3 majority in the parliament till the last moment in case they need to pass some pro-alliance bills. Also, they want to keep their majority to pull Article 6 against General Pervez Musharraf who is expected to reach Pakistan anytime to kick-off his political campaign as a silent majority is waiting to bring him back in the next elections to restore the conditions similar to what prevailed during his regime. They are also afraid that PTI and APML with their honest and

43

capable leaderships may join hands in elections against PPP and PML-N who have already failed to govern three times in the past and people of Pakistan are desperately looking for a change. A recent poll by PEW Research Center on June 27, 2012 places Imran Khan as the most popular leader and General Pervez Musharraf the fourth most popular political leader above President Zardari and former Prime Minister Yousuf Raza Gilani. The same poll shows Sharif and Chaudhary declining in their popularity since 2010.

Article 224 of Constitution of Pakistan stipulates the creation of a caretaker government before elections, but does not stipulate the time period allowed to the caretaker government to manage free and fair elections. The last four caretaker governments reveal that the minimum time given to Ghulam Mustafa Jatio in 1990 was 68 days and maximum time allowed to Mian Mohammad Soomro in 2008 was 94 days. The recent discovery by SC that the current voters lists have over 3 crores (30 million) *jaali* (false) voters while over 4 crores (40 million) genuine voters are not even listed is a troubling news. If these facts are correct, it is absolutely clear that Honorable Fakhruddin G. Ibrahim will take much more time than taken during the 1990 and 2008 elections. Also, the current chaotic state in the country needs to be normalized by bringing the law and order situation in the country under control before any peaceful elections can take place. Most of the political observers feel that three months may not be enough for a caretaker government to normalize the conditions which are already in deep disarray and not conducive for next elections in the country. There are suggestions from certain quarters that, to create an environment conducive for elections, an interim government based on "Bangladesh model" be set up. There is, however, a general consensus in political circles that the President must dissolve the parliament immediately to appoint a caretaker government to avoid further deterioration of and anarchy in Pakistan. The interim government then should gain the confidence of people and politicians to establish a peaceful environment conducive for free and fair elections.

Unlike the selection of CEC, the selection of the head of the caretaker government is more complex and must meet the expectations of people, political parties, SC and the establishment. The 20th Amendment passed by the parliament recently requires assurances from the government (PPP) to its friendly opposition (PML-N) to appoint an impartial caretaker set-up. In a highly politicized environment in Pakistan where all known politicians and bureaucrats are aligned to political parties in active politics, it is hard to find a neutral head of interim government acceptable not only to PPP and PML-N (who may form an alliance themselves in the upcoming elections) but also to real opposition parties such as PTI, APML and AML who are not in parliament but enjoy high popularity amongst the voters. By convention a caretaker prime minister simply runs the affairs of state such as law and order situation, security of state and its citizens, compliance with international commitments and day to day needs of the people, etc. in the interim till the new parliament is elected. However, being the head of the government, he is also expected to ensure free and fair elections by providing CEC with the tools they need in the elections.

The free and fair election can only be held if CEC and the Interim Prime Minister (IPM) and his cabinet are honest, impartial and strong to reject all interferences and irregularities in the elections. Every one of us has faith in Fakhruddin G. Ibrahim, CEC, who is an honest administrator and would not allow any rigging or corruption. However, for IPM the clock is still ticking and some observers are taking the names of Asma Jehangir and Abdullah Hussain Haroon to head the interim government. While Asma Jehangir is a respectable name for the job her involvement as a lawyer in PPP cases disqualifies her for the job of IPM. Abdullah Hussain Haroon, on the other hand, is a person who carries no "political baggage" but is still aligned with PPP and served in their government as speaker of Sindh Assembly and was posted by PPP to General Assembly as Pakistan's delegate. Since IPM represents a symbol and a message nationally and internationally it is important that the person appointed as IPM should not only be impartial but he/she should also be perceived as impartial. With my limited knowledge about the non-aligned persons in Pakistan, I can suggest a few neutral persons who are well known and could make a good IPM such as Dr. Shams Kassim-Lakha, former President and CEO of Agha Khan University, Dr. Adil Najam, Vice Chancellor of Lahore University of Management Sciences, and Abdus Sattar Edhi, a well known philanthropist extraordinaire and an excellent administrator. IPM must also decide a cabinet which must consist of non-aligned persons, some of them can be engaged from the overseas Pakistanis such as Tariq Javed, Senior advisor to SAMA (Saudi Arabia Monetary Agency), Lord Nazir Ahmed, member of House of Lords (UK), Dr. Khalid Luqman Chaudhry, President, PAC (USA), Aysha Ejaz Khan, lawyer and activist women's rights (USA), Burhan Khan, Chairman, Overseas Pakistani Forum and President of Friends of Pakistan in Calgary (Canada) and many more.

President Asif Ali Zardari in last four and half years of his democratic rule has introduced a new form of politics in configuring the governance, which I brand as a "Coalition of Comfort" (COC). As we all know, PPP, the majority party in parliament, invited other parties in parliament and offered them to join COC by offering political favors, privileges, ministries as well as funds to fulfill their personal agendas, not that of their voters or the people of Pakistan. Under COC concept, PPP initially created alliances with PML-N and ANP but later MQM, JUI and PML-Q have also joined this alliance; leaving the elected parliament practically with no opposition. This made the governing alliances worse than a "dictator" because a self imposed dictator can be criticized for not being democratic but democratically elected dictators cannot be questioned for any of their ill doings since they are elected by the people.

Ali Abbas Hasanie addressing the crowd assembled for the inauguration of a cricket tournament with Madam Louise Harel, Leader of the Official Opposition at the City of Montreal and Leader of Vision Montreal. Photo courtesy of office of Leader of Vision Montreal

In four and half years of democratic rule, the political parties and their leaders in parliament fulfilled their personal goals and the goals of their associates in becoming richer but the country and the people of country have reached to the brink of bankruptcy and are paying dearly through their sufferings of no jobs, no electricity, unbearable high prices for items of necessities and complete break-down of law and order to provide security and safety to the citizens. No one can believe that these governing alliances are again claiming victory in the next elections based on their "vote banks" of the people who are already crushed by them. These leaders of COC are hoping that the people will vote for them again because they have not changed their allegiance with the leaders and the party, who cheated them, drowned them and crushed them. Hello fellow citizens! It is time to cross the floor and break all allegiances without any fear to defeat COC parties and bring honest and capable leadership to salvage the country which is in an extremely critical state.

While the internal situation in the country is going from bad to worse, the national security of Pakistan is also being challenged by many corners including the USA. The introduction of motion by US Congressman Dana Rohrabacher co-sponsored by House Representatives Louie Gohmert and Steve King calling upon Pakistan to recognize the right to self-determination by Baluchistan is a clear violation of international rules and a direct meddling in the affairs of a sovereign state. Although Obama administration had assured Islamabad that it is committed to the unity and integrity of Pakistan, Dana Rohrabacher and the House Representatives in moving their resolution did not take into consideration that the people of Baluchistan are firmly with Pakistan (refer to General Pervez Musharraf's recent two parts article in Lahore Times on Baluchistan). One wonders if the House of Representatives ever supported the right to self-determination by Kashmiris who are fighting for their freedom since 1947. Do we know why foreign powers are meddling in the affairs of Pakistan; of course because they know that the people of Pakistan are fed up with corrupt politicians and the current abysmal living conditions and perhaps in their opinion, may support any movement which can free them from these corrupt and self-serving politicians in taking them out of the current condition.

My observation based on current situation is that the elections will be between parties known as *status quo* parties in parliament (COC) such as PPP, PML-N, PML-Q, ANP, MQM & JUI and the parties which are not in the parliament but are known as parties for "change" such as PTI, APML & AML who are quickly gaining ground in public opinion polls and whose leaders are considered as honest and capable of salvaging the critical situation faced by the nation today.

The four and half years of democratic anarchy has opened the eyes of the people of Pakistan who will use their votes to reject all parties in COC and elect non-parties to bring change; change for the betterment of the people of Pakistan. It is widely predicted that if non-*status quo* parties, which are high in opinion polls, lose the elections due to corruption and rigging; the election results would be rejected by the people and protests will fill the streets in a much worse way than the 1977 elections which were claimed to be rigged by PPP. That is why, for the sake of Pakistan, it is of primordial importance that Chief Election Commissioner and the caretaker Prime Minister and his cabinet must be impartial, sincere, committed, capable and of extra-ordinary merit.

References

Published in The Lahore Times: August 7, 2012
Published in World News Network: September 2, 2012

SC's decision on dual nationals contradicts the fundamental rights granted to citizens by constitution

The Supreme Court's ruling on Thursday disqualifying dual national citizens is a contradiction of fundamental rights granted to citizens under Article 25 of the Constitution of Pakistan. Article 25 provides that all citizens are equal before law and are entitled to equal protection of law. The dual national citizens who hold Pakistani passport and National Identity Card are true citizens of Pakistan and therefore have the right to vote in the general elections in Pakistan. In case of a contradiction in law by virtue of Article 63(1)(c), if narrowly interpreted, the provisions of Fundamental Rights under Article 25 (1) should prevail over Article 63(1)(c). The Supreme Court is aware that Article 8 of the constitution declares the laws inconsistent with or in derogation of fundamental rights to be void.

Dr. Babar Awan's plea that the law about dual nationality contradicts Article 8 of the constitution is not true; on the contrary Article 8 will be contradicted if a citizen of Pakistan is discriminated on the basis of his/her dual nationality. The political leaders who are against the dual nationals taking part in the elections are afraid that dual national candidates with their skills, honesty and dedication may outsmart their candidates in the elections.

According to Pakistan Citizenship Act 1951 (as amended in 1952, 1972, 1973 and 2000) a citizen of Pakistan shall cease to be citizen of Pakistan if he is at the same time a citizen or national of any other country except that the law allows Pakistan citizen to hold dual nationality of sixteen (16) countries which include U.K., France, United States, Canada, Switzerland, Australia, Netherlands, Belgium, Italy and others. Due to this provision of law, ECP does not discriminate the citizens with dual nationality and allow them to vote in the elections. The question then arises, if a citizen of Pakistan is allowed the right to vote then why the same citizen is not allowed to be a parliamentarian?

Those against the dual nationals to take part in the elections often bring the argument that the allegiance of a dual national Pakistani is suspicious. These misguided groups of people are not aware that the loyalty of overseas Pakistanis for Pakistan living in foreign lands is much at par if not above those living in Pakistan. They are the first line of defense for Pakistan as they stand firm against the opponents of Pakistan in foreign lands for the sovereignty, integrity, solidarity, well being and prosperity of Pakistan. The allegiance of dual nationals for Pakistan cannot be comprised by the allegiance given by them to a foreign country for the reason of dual nationality as these dual nationals fight everyday on the streets of foreign countries for Pakistan with their foreign governments and policy makers if they show any antagonism, unfriendliness or conflict against Pakistan.

The position paper prepared by Pakistan Institute of Legislative Development and Transparency (PILDAT) gave eight reasons for not granting the right to dual nationals to take part in the elections which are superfluous and full of unfounded assumptions and fears; such as a conflict of interest would not allow a dual national in Pakistani parliament to vote against NATO—Pakistani dual nationals demonstrate everyday on the streets of the USA, UK and Europe against the brutality of NATO in Pakistan; or a dual national's fate is not tied to the fate of Pakistan therefore allowing them to be on driver's seat can be detrimental to the interests of Pakistan—without being on driver's seat Pakistanis are working everyday for the well-being of Pakistan and Pakistanis—check with philanthropists. PILDAT's position paper is based on unfounded facts and shallow thinking and far from the reality of the concept that the world has now become a global village and the residents of this global village have full allegiance with their home lands whatever their homeland is

References

Published in The Lahore Times: September 21, 2012
Published in World News Network: October 2, 2012
Published in The Kooza: September 21, 2012

Is time running out for free and fair elections in Pakistan?

On Wednesday, October 3, 2012, Mr. Qamar Zaman Kaira, the Federal Minister for Information and Broadcasting, stated on a television channel that the "Elections would be held on time and care-taker government would be put in place on March 18, 2013". Prior to that, on September 28, 2012, while discussing the formation of a care-taker government, the same Minister gave a statement that the "consultation is a constitutional requirement and we will consult our allies, opposition parties and even those parties who do not have representation in parliament". Is there any truth to these statements?

The ground reality in Pakistan today is that sadly the country is in a major turmoil and distress while becoming a dysfunctional state as each day races past us. Mr. Kaira's wishful thinking that the government will be able to manage peaceful general elections in mere 60 days is beyond comprehension and defies any logic. Pakistan has become a country where the law and order situation has totally collapsed and been trampled, while target killings, *bhatta khori (*ransom), abduction and the brazen day-light robberies of the citizens' homes have all become the order of the day.

It is a country where there is no writ of the government and the sectarian violence, atrocities and heinous crimes are at an all time high. It is a country whose economy is in dire straits while the poverty is spreading like a cancer killing the low and middle class citizens along with their hopes and ambitions. It is a country that is in constant unrest internally as the foreign powers are watching it closely to target its nuclear program. It is a country that is being ruled by parties of corrupt and dishonest politicians who are blatantly lying and misleading the people of Pakistan to get themselves elected back to the power, for their own personal motives and gains, despite their dismal records of governance in the past for more than once.

Ali Abbas Hasanie speaking at a symposium organized in Montreal, Canada on Malala Yousufzai Photo courtesy of Weekly Ummeed newspaper Montral, Canada

Mr. Kaira is legally correct when he says that Article 224 (1) provides that the general elections must take place within 60 days immediately following the day on which the term of the elected government is due to expire (i.e. March 18, 2013), which in return makes the last date of elections as May 17, 2013. However, Article 224 (2) provides that upon the dissolution of the national assembly, the elections shall be held within a period of 90 days which means that the ECP may demand an additional 30 days (considering the present state of affairs in the country) to complete the polls. Furthermore, Article 224 (2) also provides that the results of the elections shall be declared no later than 14 days after the conclusion of the polls; therefore the polling has to be concluded by May 3, 2013 in order to meet the deadline of May 17, 2013, and to avoid the automatic dissolution of the parliament. If my understanding of the constitution is correct, then the President must dissolve the parliament no later than February 3, 2013, and not on March 18, 2013, as announced by Mr. Kaira.

There are roughly five months left from now till March 18, 2013 when the clock of the 60 days time will start ticking to set up a caretaker government, and roughly six and a half months to set up the polling date on or before May 3, 2013. The political pundits who are watching the sensitive conditions in the country believe that a minimum of six months time will be required to create a peaceful and stable environment and to settle issues that re critical to peaceful and impartial elections in Pakistan. These issues are as follows:

1. To bring the law and order situation under control with tight monitoring whereby the political campaigns can safely and fairly be organized while the voters can fearlessly and securely go to the polling stations to cast their votes. It is believed that there is major unrest in Baluchistan, FATA and some parts of KPK. And according to some observers peaceful elections in these areas are almost near impossible.

2. To establish a voters list which is absolutely error-free and unbiased to the mutual satisfaction of all the parties and individuals involved. Honorable Fakhruddin G. Ibrahim has released the voters list, which roughly contains 84.4 million voters. This list has apparently the entries of about 30 million *jaali* (counterfeit) voters and about 40 million or so missing voters, as was identified earlier by the Election Commission. However, these corrections need to be verified and confirmed by all the political parties and individuals before elections.

3. To vigilantly revisit all the criteria for the nomination of the candidates for the elections in light of the constitutional provisions. The criteria exclude the citizens with dual nationality, which is a dilemma that may perhaps require extensive inquiries and verifications from the foreign governments. Currently, there are elected members in the parliament who are dual nationals but only a few of them have been identified and disqualified.

4. To rule on the petition against the SPLGO on the grounds that an ordinance cannot overrule the sanctity of an Act passed by the assembly.

5. To clarify the electoral expenditures as allowed by the ECP in the face of allegations that the mainstream parties have already engaged with the prominent media for the elections purposes by paying substantial amounts.

6. Above all, the petitions filed by the political parties on constitutional and non-constitutional grounds in the courts which are directly related to the elections, need to be resolved before the date of the nomination is announced i.e., NRO cases which involve the misappropriation of funds against politicians expected to be taking part in the elections, Air Marshal (Retd) Asghar Khan's petition alleging senior politicians involved in bribery, petitions against the disqualification of dual national parliamentarians and perhaps many more.

You may recall that the country was abruptly thrown into a political campaign mode when PML-N removed the PPP ministers from the Punjab government in February of 2011, and had severely criticized the record of the PPP government in dealing with the issues in the country. This campaign had further heated up when the politicians such as Javed Hashmi, Kursheed Mahmood Qasuri, Shah Mahmood Qureshi and Jahangir Khan Tareen, joined Pakistan Tehrik-e-Insaf whose leader Imran Khan was already in the midst of campaigning for the next elections while attracting large crowds in major cities. In other words, all the major parties are already in active and deep campaigning since the beginning of 2011 except the fact that the PPP and its allies are not comfortable with their chance of victory in the elections and therefore are using all sorts of tactics to delay the elections till the very last moment. It is very rare for a country which is in a major turmoil to sustain a year and a half of political campaigns while leaving a troubled country in limbo for that long!

While the electioneering is in process since February 2011, the ruling alliance is dragging its feet to dissolve the parliament and sort out the critical issues to allow a caretaker set-up to level the ground for the upcoming elections. If we look closely at the critical issues, it appears that even a six months period is simply not enough to resolve them. It seems as if some of these issues, although related to the elections, may be put aside by the interim government in order to hold the elections within the time allowed by the constitution. However, the SC may intervene in holding the general elections before all the critical and unresolved issues relating to elections are settled by the deliberation in the SC or by taking *a suo motu* action.

Most observers strongly feel that if the caretaker set-up is not swiftly announced by the President before the end of October this year, then, shockingly enough, the time will run out for free and fair elections in Pakistan. The parliament may then hit the provisions of Article 48 (2) where the President shall be required under the constitution to dissolve the parliament and refer the matter under Article 58 (3) to the SC and the SC shall decide the reference within 30 days and whose decision shall be final

It is generally acknowledged that the SC will not allow the holding of the general elections till the critical court decisions directly related to the general elections are disposed of by the SC. The disposing of these cases may go well beyond the last date as established under Article 52 of the constitution i.e., May 17, 2013. If this happens and the date of elections can not be fixed before the due date, the President then would have no choice but to dissolve the interim government, cancel the general elections announced earlier, and notify the SC under Article 58(3) of the constitution. The SC may then appoint an interim set-up and wait to announce the date of elections until and unless all the cases are resolved and a peaceful environment exists for the general elections. In other words, this is a replica of the Bangladesh Model which most of the political parties in Pakistan are not in favor of by any means.

On Friday, October 6, 2012, the Sindh High Court (SHC) directed the provincial government of Sindh to submit comments within two weeks regarding the delay in conducting the local body elections in its province. Lately, President has also started the rhetoric of holding local government polls in Sindh before the general elections which some experts sense as foul play and yet another ploy of the government to delay the general elections. Let us presume for a moment, that in complying with the SHC order, the government of Sindh decides to hold the local bodies' elections in the month of October. According to the ECP, if requests for the local bodies' elections are sent to them, say sometime in October sometime, then under the law, the ECP would be allowed to organize the polls within 90 days or by January 2013. This would mean that the appointment of the interim set-up for general elections would be postponed till February 2013. This means that the interim government would have a period of three months or less to complete the general elections and announce the results before May 3, 2013, a task which seems to be not attainable considering the dire situation of Pakistan.

The history in Pakistan is a witness that any controversial affair organized by the government through an ordinance comes under severe attack by the general public. The most recent examples of which are the NRO, the ordinance to give constitutional protection to the PM and other ministers, SPLGO, etc. These ordinances have been fervently challenged in the SC. For example, on September 28, Advocate Mumtaz Lashari, filed a petition against the SPLGO while the Supreme Court took *suo Motu* on NRO and the ordinance to give constitutional protection to the PM and ministers. There is likelihood that once the interim government is in power and the SC strikes down SPLGO, the President at that point would have no choice but to order the governor of Sindh to repeal the ordinance and disband the local bodies if the elections have already been held under SPLGO. This process will further cause unwarranted delays in holding the general elections, notwithstanding that the President under the constitution is required to dissolve national assembly and appoint the interim government with a date of the general elections no later than May 3, 2013. The appointment of the care-taker government under the constitution and in the light of Amendment

20 presents a new dilemma where the President is required under Article 224 (1A) to consult with the prime minister and the leader of opposition in appointing the interim Prime Minister. But nowhere in the constitution does it state that the President is legally bound by the result of such consultation or nomination except on moral grounds. Amendment 20 on the other hand, provides a long drawn procedure to come up with a name to appoint an interim Prime Minister but nowhere, in my opinion, does it mention that the constitutional right of the President to appoint the interim Prime Minister is taken away and instead given to a committee or ECP.

The PPP and its allies are hoping that in delaying the dissolution of the assembly, a major chaos might erupt in the country and either the SC or the establishment may act to cause a dissolution of the assembly. If this ever happens, then they will once again get a chance to go to the people "under the pretext of mercy for the unconstitutional demise of a democratically elected assembly" and will demand the people to rescue the democracy as they did the last time. Senior observers are of the opinion that both the Army and the SC have learned their lessons and this will not happen unless a severe emergency occurs as a result of, for example, a military attack on Pakistan by foreign powers after which the President decides to dissolve the parliament to set up an interim government with a prominent presence of army personnel under the Emergency rule.

The other view is that the PPP and their allies are waiting for an opportunity to enhance their popularity, such as the SC decision on Asghar Khan's petition, since the latest IRS polls suggest a downtrend in the popularity of PTI as a major force to bring about the change in the country. While the reason for the decline in popularity of PTI may be directly associated with the disgruntled politicians in his party, it is true that Imran's grassroots approach to portray PTI as a truly democratic party is turning out to be a terrible mistake which is creating all kinds of divisions in his party. However, such delaying tactics will never gain any significant popularity for PPP or PML-N as the people clearly blame these two parties for the destruction of Pakistan.

If the President does not dissolve the parliament in October but waits till March 18, 2013, to appoint the caretaker government, then the caretaker government will not only fail to restore the law and order but will also fail to resolve the critical issues due to any unforeseen reasons such as an increase in militancy, attacks on the government properties, an increase in the sectarian violence, unwanted activities on our borders, etc. The holding of these elections will then become impossible by May 17, 2013 and this will again lead to a situation whereby the President will be obliged to refer the matter to the SC who may cancel all the elections and may seek the help of technocrats, bureaucrats and the establishment to run the affairs of the state till the new parliament is elected and installed in the country. This action would not be viewed quite as democratic but no one except for the government, the politicians and the political parties both in the government and outside the government will be blamed for this unfortunate outcome.

Pakistan under the democratically elected parliament is disgustingly going through some very difficult and unwarranted circumstances. The people of Pakistan, who are constantly facing the brunt of the government atrocities and missteps and bear the burden, are suffering from misery, corruption, poverty, insecurity, killings, injustices and above all downright humiliation. Majority of the people are now demanding immediate general elections and earnestly looking at the establishment and the SC to find some way to force the President to dissolve the current government and appoint an interim setup.

There is a constant power play between the government and the SC and two majority parties in the parliament have threatened to bring Article 6 to the forefront, if anyone dares to unseat them from the parliament. Barrister Aitzaz Ahsan Chaudhri has already reminded the SC that they have no jurisdiction over the executive power of the government under the constitution. This means that any verdict by the SC to call for an immediate general election may simply be ignored by the government and tossed aside. The people of Pakistan arguably have not seen a bigger fraud in the history of Pakistan, as HasanNisar rightfully puts it, than the present democratically elected 'dictators' under the façade of democracy.

Imran Khan and his PTI are gaining ground amongst the young and old voters and deserve to be the part of the "change" which the nation is seriously looking for. It is believed that of the four million new voters added to the voters list, a majority of them are for the "change". People are looking back in the past and rehashing the days of General Pervez Musharraf's government when the law and order, economic prosperity, homeland security and the foreign diplomacy were at their best in the recent past in Pakistan. While almost all known party leaders and their party members are associated with huge corruption, dishonesty and the lack of leadership, both Imran Khan and General Pervez Musharraf are viewed as honest, passionate and strong leaders to rescue the country from the current crises.

The people of Pakistan are desperately looking for "change" in government; the government of corrupt and dishonest leaders and their party members. And it is no secret any more who those corrupt and dishonest leaders are—go to the list of "NRO" and the verdict of Air Marshall Asghar Khan's case by the SC, and check the petitions filed against the corruptions of the leaders and their associates of major political parties in the SC. The Chief Elections Commissioner Honorable Fakhruddin G. Ibrahim in his message to the nation said "*Bhai kal jakar vote zaroor karna—voting kay duaran ham tumhari safety aur security ki zamanat detey hain*" (Please do go for vote—we guarantee your safety and security during polling).

Some senior political analyst fervently believe that the upcoming elections will be an election between the *status-quo* parties who are currently in the parliament and are responsible for the present disastrous and atrocious situation in the country; and the parties which are not in the government but want to bring about the "change" that Pakistan and its citizens so deeply deserve.

This means that the PPP and PML-N and their allies or so-called the *status-quo* parties, will probably form an election alliance while the PTI and APML and their allies or so-called the parties for "change" may form another alliance in the elections. With the strong, charismatic and honest leadership of Imran Khan and General Pervez Musharraf, the people of Pakistan will support the new ideas of Imran Khan and the tested leadership of General Pervez Musharraf. It is about time that the people must put the interest of Pakistan first and foremost, and finally raise themselves above all other loyalties by breaking the barriers which divide them in the elections.

Hasan Nisar is right that the current democracy in Pakistan is the biggest fraud against the people of Pakistan who are innocent victims of present regime. But we must keep in mind that it is not the democracy at fault, rather it is the people who are not using their "voting power," a right and a privilege, and yet are still being deceived by the usual hollow slogans and false statements of failed politicians and their egotistical political parties. It goes without saying that Pakistan is in deep trouble right now, as everything looks dismal. However it is not without hope. And the only solution is that people wake up today, face the reality, go to the polling stations and use the power of vote for "change".

References

Published in The Lahore Times: October 25, 2012
Published in World News Network: October 28, 2012

Democracy under corrupt politicians is a fraud against people of Pakistan

Voters must defeat corrupt politicians to bring the needed change in Pakistan

On March 18, 2013, the current elected parliament will complete its five-year term. An overview of this five-year period of a democratically elected government discloses the fact that during this period, Pakistan unfortunately has lost its stability and has fallen backwards in time, while the anarchy in the country has reached to such an extreme that there is absolutely no law and order in the country. Killings, abductions, ransoms, robberies—and the list goes on—have made the lives of ordinary people miserable, a living hell to say the very least. Unemployment is at its peak and poverty and hunger have forced innocent people to commit suicide.

The basic necessities of life that is the right of all humans such as food, water, electricity and gas are either not available or they are beyond the reach of an average citizen. Corruption, murder and violence have spread like a cancer in the society while flames of continue to gnaw at the very soul of this nation. Businesses and investments are all fleeing away from the country leaving the economy in a big shamble. Major institutions such as the Government, the Army, the Judiciary and the National Accountability Bureau are in a major conflict and the country is on the brink of bankruptcy.

The fact remains that Pakistan that was once the pride of the whole nation has today become the embarrassment only due to a corrupt few who have brazenly taken the country hostage through the thin veil of democracy. The question then arises—does Pakistan or its people deserve democracy? The answer is an absolute '*Yes*'! But not the same democracy that prevails in the country today, suffocating it in the process and depriving it of its resources, potential and a future. Far from it. Why? The answer is quite clear and very simple. It is because the current so-called democracy that exists today under the corrupt politicians is nothing but a fraud and a joke against the people of Pakistan. So who then we blame for imposing this fraud on us? Whose fault it is that Pakistan is withering away along with the dreams and hopes of its 180 million citizens who are dying a thousands deaths each and every day. Regrettably, it is the '*voters*' who have put these corrupt politicians in power.

We are well aware that before this democratically elected government, we had a nine-year period that was governed by so-called dictator General Pervez Musharraf. During his term, the history will attest to this fact, generally the people had a peaceful and prosperous life full of aspirations and hope. The country at that time was making huge progress and taking immense strides, which has been confirmed by various national and international institutions. One can easily verify this fact by simply comparing today's situation in any sector against that of just five years ago.

The politicians in the last elections have clearly exploited a few instances such as the NRO, Lal Masjid, the death of Sardar Bugti as well as the Chief Justice incident and as a result have gotten themselves elected to power. Now we must ask ourselves—*Have we learned any lesson from such a major setback to the country by electing corrupt politicians as we watch silently the destruction and plundering of our own nation?*

Constitutionally, Pakistan is a democratic nation in which the people directly elect the Parliament, which is a House of Representatives consisting of 336 individuals of which 266 are directly elected from across the country. If these individuals or at least the majority of them are honest, capable, committed and sincerely care for the country above anything else, then rest assured, you will have good and viable governance which will entail, prosperity, peace, justice and happiness for Pakistan and the people of Pakistan with a strong and positive hope for better future. I am confident that Pakistan will have a brighter and better tomorrow, *Insha Allah* under honest, proficient and sincere leadership elected by the people and for the people.

On the other hand, if the elected politicians turn out to be corrupt, dishonest, incompetent and self-serving, then sadly you will witness something even worse than what we are all seeing today. Pakistan is quickly moving towards destruction due to the corrupt politicians who have set a pathetic example that puts everything to shame.

Politicians in Pakistan have successfully implanted into the minds of the people that democracy is the only way for Pakistan to solve its problems and rid itself of the chains of tribulations. Without any doubt, democracy is indeed the best system which the free world has so far established, but has it solved the problems of Pakistan and its citizens? The answer is a resounding NO! We have a democratically elected government in Pakistan for almost five years now. All the major parties of Pakistan i.e., PPP, PML-N, PML-Q, MQM, ANP and JUI-F are in the parliament except for PTI, APML and PAML. The question then arises if the democracy is the best system and solution, then why is our country with its people, suffering under this democratic system. The answer is clear and simple.

The prerequisites of any democracy must exist in the country in order for democracy to be working 'for the people' of any democratic country. In my previous article, dated January 16, 2012, titled "Next general election is a test of people's power in Pakistan," I clearly identified three key elements that make a democratic system work; namely: *(1) The Voters, (2) The Elections and (3) The Leaders with their political parties.* In the last sixty years of our history, unfortunately, we have totally failed in all these key elements. The voters did not participate in large numbers, and those who did participate were not voting for the betterment of the country through their conscience but instead voted either under coercion or to please their friends or *biradari.* The elections were not free and fair by any means as confirmed by the latest verdict by the SC in the Asghar Khan Petition, which is just the tip of an iceberg witnessing this ugly fact. And the most important point that simply can not be ignored is that the elected leaders and their parties were not honest, capable and sincere in most cases.

In February of 2008, when the last elections were taking place in the country, all the necessary information about the two major parties elected in the parliament were available to the voters. This included the detailed information that the current ruling party had formed the government four times in the past while its government had been dissolved twice by the President due to its blatant corruption and deliberate abuse of power. And it did not end there. There were and are numerous cases against them in the court for corruption. Also, the so-called official opposition in the parliament had formed the government two times in the center and five times in the province of Punjab.

And it too was dissolved by the President once due to its own corruption and misuse of power. And there were and are numerous cases against them in the court on their corruption and crimes as well. Their leader, who is still leading the party, has been convicted and jailed. The BBC ran a documentary called "Correspondent" in 1999 on their corruption just before the military coup took place in October. With all these facts lingering in the public knowledge, our corrupt politicians in 2008 were still surprisingly able to convince the voters about their supposed 'honesty' and got themselves elected back to power! *What a tragedy indeed and yet another sad day for Pakistan and its citizens!*

After five years in power, there is nothing better at all to report by these elected parties who are in the parliament except for the consistent horror stories of corruption, lawlessness, killings, hunger and violence all across the country and mostly in the city of Karachi. The National Accountability Bureau (NAB) has recently released a report on the daily corruption of Rs. 7-8 arab (Rs. 7 billion) which the Federal cabinet obviously has rejected. A federal minister is quoted as saying that with only Rs. 25.20 trillion in the annual national revenue, a daily corruption of Rs 7-8 billion or an annual corruption of Rs. 2.55 trillion or 10% is not possible. *I would say that the minister is underestimating the power of corruption in the country!*

The history has once again proven itself right, as the leaders of most of the ruling parties are seen in the forefront when it comes to the corruption and mismanagement of the country. This is a disturbing fact that must be recognized by the voters and addressed before it's too late, if it is not already. These parties known as *status quo* parties are absurdly and shamelessly campaigning again for reelection despite serious allegations against them which include corruption, mismanagement and complete failure to govern. To the surprise of the intellectuals and the democratic world, it appears from the recent public opinion polls that unfortunately these corrupt politicians are getting away once again by blatantly misleading people through their candid lies just to reelect themselves back to power.

All kinds of alliances are being formed between the corrupt politicians with all sorts of tactics being played out at the cost of the country. This is just to recapture the power once again for their own benefit to enjoy the corruption while punishing the innocent citizens. The noble advice from the well-wishers and the concerned friends of Pakistan to voters is not to be misled by the false statements and deceitful acts of these corrupt politicians since they have brought the country to the brink of a failed state as they continue to wreak havoc. The only way these corrupt politicians can be stopped from going to the Parliament is by the very voters, defeating them hands down in the next elections and finally throwing them out of power permanently.

Dr. Tahir-ul Qadri an honest and noble politician as well as an Islamic scholar is launching a campaign against the corrupt politicians and the corrupt political system in Pakistan. He recently appeared on many talk shows and unveiled the facts about the democracy in Pakistan and the dishonest political leaders and their parties. He very strongly appealed to the voters in Pakistan not to elect the *status quo* politicians in the next elections as their re-election would be a serious mistake and would result in the demise of Pakistan. He has called a public meeting on December 23rd at the Minar-e-Pakistan. I strongly suggest that the voters must attend this meeting or at least listen to his message.

Most of the observers believe that there are two prominent leaders whose honesty, sincerity and commitment cannot be questioned in Pakistan, and they are the best solution for Pakistan's future. *One is Imran Khan and his PTI.* The voters must give him and his party a chance to bring about the change and a new hope in the country. I firmly support Imran Khan with his mission and agree with the fact that the corruption can definitely be beaten in 90 days. Personally, I would say that it could be beaten on the very day when you place honest and competent people in the highest office, i.e., the cabinet and the bureaucracy of the government.

The other leader who has clearly demonstrated his honesty and capability and strength and has run Pakistan successfully beyond any doubt is General Pervez Musharraf of APML. My sincere advice to the people of Pakistan is not to listen to the baseless comments against him using such words as "dictator" or an "army man" as these are ridiculous, rather groundless accusations to say the least in order to keep him and his party away from contesting the next elections. General Musharraf has already proven his worth, has vividly displayed his honesty and commitment to Pakistan and its citizens, as a statesman when he ran this country under a democratically elected government of PML-Q and brought peace and happiness into the lives of people during his regime. Enormous development had taken place in all sectors of Pakistan during his regime, which all the national and international sources have already confirmed. There is absolutely nothing wrong if a man with a military background, after his retirement from the army, runs for a public office.

There are many examples in the world where a person with an army background has democratically become the head of state or the government which include Dwight D. Eisenhower of the USA who was a 5 star General in the US army and was the Commander of the Allied Forces in the Second World War, Charles de Gaulle of France who was an Army General in French Army in Second world war, Sir Winston Churchill of U.K. who was an Officer in the British Army as well as George Washington, the first President of the USA who was the Commander in Chief of the Continental Army. If these army men could lead the powerful democracies of the world, then why can Pakistan not elect General Pervez Musharraf to power?

There is no doubt in my mind that the people of Pakistan are fully aware of the issues confronting Pakistan and the people of Pakistan. It is high time to use the "Voters Power" to save Pakistan and guard its future by electing honest, capable and tested leaders and their parties to power. It is long overdue, and the time is now! Do not stand by idle while Pakistan your country is being disgustingly pillaged and destroyed by the corrupt politicians. The words of wisdom for Imran Khan, General Pervez Musharraf and other honest and committed leaders are that you must recognize that the shrewd gangs of corrupt politicians are making all kinds of alliances against all of you. Now it is the chance for you to put aside your personal pride and differences and instead join hands in the next elections to defeat these corrupt and incompetent politicians for the common goal of Pakistan, its stability and future. People have faith and confidence in both Imran Khan and General Pervez Musharraf who are honest, experienced, capable and trusted and their alliance would certainly bring the needed and overdue "change" in Pakistan.

References

Published The Lahore Times: December 21, 2012
Published in The Kooza: December 20, 2012

Dual nationality of Pakistanis does not contradict the constitution

*Masses must join Dr. Tahir-ul Qadri's Long
March to change corrupt political system*

The historical public meeting of Dr. Tahir-ul-Qadri at Minar-e-Pakistan on December 23, 2012 has triggered a heated debate over the role of overseas Pakistanis in the affairs of Pakistan. These unwanted debates are a deliberate attempt to divert the attention of public from the core issues of corrupt political system and the corrupt political practices by the corrupt and dishonest politicians to seize power in the upcoming elections in Pakistan. I am closely watching the interviews and talk shows of Dr. Tahir-ul Qadri and am highly disappointed at how corrupt politicians and their supporters have launched the character assassination of a "noble man" with a "noble mission" by propagating irrelevant and deceitful information to dodge the core issue of "corruption" in the elections in Pakistan.

Let us first deal with the residency issue of overseas Pakistanis and their dual nationality. The Constitution of Pakistan does not impose any residential limitation on the citizens of Pakistan whether they live within the boundaries of Pakistan or outside. Today, the world is a global village and all free citizens on earth have a right to live, to earn a living, to get education, to do business, to conduct research or to enjoy the benefits offered by the resident countries, without disassociating themselves from their motherland. Some of the great revolutionary leaders of the world such as Ayatollah Khomeini, Jalaluddin Afghani, Mao Zedong, Mohandas Gandhi, and Fidel Castro had lived outside their home countries and upon the return to their homeland they brought the greatest revolutions of their time all for the right reasons.

Ali Abbas Hasanie speaking on the role of Media in the society at Weekly Umeed's inauguration in Montreal Canada Photo Weekly Umeed newspaper

A person who lives in Sindh has a right to raise his voice against the injustices to his fellow citizens in Punjab; a person who is a resident in Khyber Pakhtunkhwa has a right to launch a protest against the brutality to his fellow citizens in Baluchistan; similarly a Pakistani citizen who lives abroad has a right to launch a campaign in Pakistan against the corrupt political systems and corrupt politicians to safeguard the rights and interest of fellow citizens in his homeland—and no one has a right to question his noble intentions on the grounds of his residency outside the country.

Some observers are raising an issue over the oath given by dual nationals to their resident countries at the time of assuming dual nationality. The Citizenship Act of Pakistan allows Pakistanis to take dual nationality of at least 16 countries without jeopardizing their Pakistani nationality. In my press release on September 21, 2012 I clarified that the allegiance given by dual national Pakistanis, to their countries of residence for the reason of obtaining dual nationality, does not compromise the allegiance for their homeland. The dual national Pakistanis fight every day on the streets of foreign countries for Pakistan with their foreign governments if their governments or the people show antagonism, unfriendliness or conflict against Pakistan. The same Pakistanis remit over $13 billion dollars annually, the second largest source of foreign exchange for Pakistan.

Apart from exploiting the residency issue, I noted that the corrupt and dishonest politicians and their supporters are constantly assassinating the character of Dr. Tahir-ul Qadri, a man who has shaken the dreams of these corrupt politicians to capture the power. These corrupt people along with some of our ignorant friends are accusing Dr. Qadri for derailing democracy, interrupting elections and over-ruling the authority of parliament and judiciary. I am shocked at how these people can misinterpret the current democracy in Pakistan which is nothing but a fraud against the people of Pakistan. The two major parties in parliament along with their allies are making the mockery of democracy, as the people of Pakistan are going through the worst time in the history of Pakistan.

I am particularly disappointed with most of our media who are unfortunately following the footsteps of our corrupt politicians and spending their time and energy in questioning Dr. Tahir-ul Qadri's honesty and truthfulness, his religious and spirituals beliefs and his residency outside Pakistan as well as the timing of his mission. Towing the old and obsolete thinking, they are trying to link his noble mission to a Western conspiracy, self-fulfillment and proxy war for the benefit of a third party which nobody knows who that party is. We as a nation have lost our faith and trust in honesty and faithfulness by living in a corrupt culture as our minds always go to negative aspects of any issue.

Let me first clear the air by stating that I do not personally know Dr. Tahir-ul Qadri, I have listened to some of his speeches on Islam and his religious beliefs but have never met him, never spoken to him in person or over the telephone and never attended any of his meetings or lectures. My only relation with him is that he is a man who has stood up against the "corruption" which is the mother of all ills in Pakistan and I am with him. As I have quoted in my last article in December 2012, democracy under corrupt politicians is a fraud against the people of Pakistan. And I commend Dr. Qadri on his wisdom and courage to take the Bull (corruption) by the horn and with the support of millions of people nib this *azab* into the bud.

For those people who are assassinating Dr. Qadri's character, I must add that from his background check up I believe he is 200% honest than all our politicians together leaving a few of them; his mission is noble and free from all political and non-political influences from internal or external sources; his slogan "save the state not the politics" is timely and is the need of the day; his wisdom to correct the political system to deter the corrupt politicians from capturing the power is "holy"; and his "Long March" to Islamabad with millions of people to force the administration to reform electoral system before the elections is truly justified.

Dr. Qadri is the voice of millions of people in Pakistan who are crushed under the corrupt rule with no law and order, no jobs, no safety, and no hope. He is a warrior who stood up to save the lives of people from cruel forces who have killed thousands and thousands of people across our land in target killings, in sectarian killings, in ransom killings, and God knows what other killings, of innocent people. Dr. Qadri's mission is simply to take the support of masses and force the government to setup an honest and independent body that can introduce electoral reforms before the elections to pave the way for free and fair elections in Pakistan. He is not against democracy, he is not against elections and he is not a candidate for any position in the interim government or a candidate in the upcoming elections. He, and I am sure all of us, want the honest and capable people to be elected in a free and fair election who can give a good governance and peaceful and prosperous living to our people.

Dr. Tahir-ul Qadri's call for a "Long March" is the only peaceful way to force the reform of a corrupt electoral system in Pakistan thereby stopping the corrupt politicians to use unlawful means to capture power; it is our national duty to join this "Long March" and bring the revolution in the country. We can do it!! China has done it, Iran has done it, Egypt has done it and now it is our turn. We must be ready to give sacrifices to bring once and for all a system that can put people's true representatives to power.

References

Published in The Lahore Times: January 12, 2013

From Islamabad bunker accord to Lahore MQ Secretariat agreement

Plutocracy system of government cedes to real democracy in Pakistan

On January 17, 2013 the plutocratic form of government in Pakistan has finally taken a positive turn towards democracy as the "people's power" under the banner of "Long March to Islamabad" led by Tahir-ul Qadri forced the Pakistan government to accept the demands of the people of Pakistan to reform the electoral system for substituting plutocracy with democracy. Shaheed Benazir Bhutto once said that democracy is the best revenge. Today the people of Pakistan want to take revenge on the elite and corrupt rulers by forcing the government to put a free and fair electoral system in place. There is unfair criticism of Qadri for staging the long march under the shield of women, children and elders. However, let me remind those critics that Qadri's choice of the long march for bringing about the change may be unusual and revolutionary, while his agenda may have been modified under the circumstances in front of D Square but nobody can dispute that his demands clearly reflect the need of the hour—transparency, accountability, equality and assurance of free and fair elections under the constitution, the rule of law and the Supreme Court judgments—all these essential elements for free and fair elections needed to bring about a change peacefully and democratically in Pakistan.

There are three major classes of governance in the world i.e., capitalism, socialism and communism. All of them are basically tied in with the economy. However, there are many forms of government under these various classes of governance ranging from monarchy, democracy, republic, dictatorship, theocracy, totalitarian, oligarchy, plutocracy and anarchy. Pakistan, which falls under the capitalism class, is unfortunately classified by the world scholars as plutocracy, which is a form of government in which elite groups govern a country for their own interests. These interests are reflected by, but are not limited to, economic interests (accumulation of wealth and privileges), a particular religious tradition (theocracy—the Taliban) or familial rule (monarchy—ancestry i.e., the family of Bhutto, Sharif). The politicians under the plutocratic form of government befool and deceive the people in the name of democracy and yet sadly no ordinary citizen can escape the stranglehold of these elite groups because they control the wealth, land, properties and jobs (mostly through corruption), and through these resourceful tools, they are unfortunately able to influence the voters and the votes. Under the bunker accord and the MQ Secretariat agreement, Qadri and his followers are trying to change this plutocracy into a much-needed democracy.

Our politicians must understand that mere holding elections in the name of democracy is not democracy since a true and honest democracy offers solutions to people's problems, which has not been the case in five years of current democratic rule in Pakistan. The country desperately needs a change, and needs it today, and unless the needed electoral reforms take place to ensure a corruption-free democratic process, the new elections would not be more than a mere "replay of corrupt elections" of the past while the democracy in Pakistan remains a dead horse being flogged by the politicians, political analysts and the esteemed journalists as usual, mostly to cater to their own hidden agendas.

Ali Abbas Hasanie in his office in Montreal, Canada

The Tahrir Square struggle of Egyptians to remove an elected dictator after 30 years has become a symbolic name for the people's democratic struggle for a "change". The question then arises, is there a Tahrir Square struggle in work in Pakistan? The corrupt politicians probably would say in their devious style, of course "not"! Let us look at it and analyze it carefully. Why would hundreds of thousands people (women, children and elders included) spend four nights under the freezing open skies of Islamabad? Why would hundreds of thousands people gather for Imran Khan at his Lahore and Karachi public meetings? How did Tahir-ul Qadri manage to gather hundreds of thousands of people at Minar-e-Pakistan on December 23? Do these events remind us of a Tahrir Square? I am sure they do, but not for the reason that someone stayed in power for too little or too long?

Lee Kuan Yew was an elected autocrat who lasted 31 long years in office but there was no Tahrir Square in Singapore. Mahathir Muhammad got elected for five consecutive terms, sometimes in controversial elections, and ruled as an elected autocrat for 22 long years but there was no Tahrir Square in Malaysia. A Tahrir Square takes place only when there is a gap between what the rulers do and what the needs of the people are. The fact remains that both Lee Kuan Yew and Mahathir Muhammad took their deprived nations and gave them prosperity and happiness through good governance. The democratically elected government of Pakistan and its friendly opposition in the parliament today has miserably failed by all accounts to fulfill the needs of the people during their five-year term, and that is why a Tahrir Square is in the making to bring about the desired change.

Qadri has never intended to derail the democracy, its process or postpone the elections but is rather fighting that the electoral reforms must be in place before the polls in order to avoid an "action replay" of the past. One can imagine that all the major parties and their allies in the parliament are claiming victory in the upcoming elections when they have a dismal record of performance in five years of democratic rule. They all know well that they are responsible for bringing Pakistan and the citizens of Pakistan to a point of disaster. But then why are they claiming victory? Because they believe that at the time of elections, all the corrupt parties will create an alliance and through their appointed interim prime minister and the election commission and through the use of corrupt elections practices, they will disrespect and defeat the honest voters and the honest chief election commissioner. The chief election commissioner, who is a sole loyal soldier without a gun in his hands, is expected to fight the rigging and the disobedience of the electoral rules by the heavyweight corrupt politicians, which in the opinion of many observers is not a realistic expectation from the chief election commissioner.

The participants of the Tahrir Square movement in Pakistan have already noticed the malicious intentions of the corrupt political parties and their leaders. They are now reacting by throwing their support behind the honest individuals such as Imran Khan, Qadri, General (Retd.) Pervez Musharraf and a few others. The people of Pakistan, to be successful in their movement, need the appointment of an honest and impartial interim prime minister along with the required electoral reforms in the light of rules and guidelines, which already exist but were not followed in the past due to the partiality of the Election Commission or for the lack of time allowed to the Election Commission of Pakistan (ECP) to verify and control the irregularities. Qadri's honest efforts through the bunker and MQ Secretariat accords are to get the electoral reforms implemented and to get the problems of appointing an honest interim PM and impartial ECP fixed.

After 65 years of experimenting with both the military and civilian regimes, the nation has reached a consensus to adopt the real and true democracy as the model of governance for Pakistan. The electoral and political doctrines under which a ruler can rig the elections through improper elections practices, through an elections committee which can bypass the electoral rules for the benefit of their chosen candidates, a federal minister who can keep 51 vehicles for his personal use and the family members of a prime minister who can engage themselves in the illicit trade or the prime minister who can divert Rs. 50 billion from the development funds to his own discretionary funds for his own personal use or for the use of his party members—all these malpractices need to be confronted and changed. There are enough lessons learned by the people of Pakistan through the Supreme Court's decision on the Asghar Khan petition and the time has arrived to rise above the conventional politics to the politics of honesty, justice, transparency and fairness. And for that reason we need a change and need it today! This change will occur only when the people of Pakistan will elect the honest and tested representatives to the parliament in upcoming elections.

The government will dissolve the parliament and announce the election date by February 6 as agreed in the MQ Secretariat agreement. Considering the fact that the government and their allies have agreed to put a constitutional face to all the decrees they have agreed to in the bunker and MQ Secretariat accords through untiring efforts of Qadri and his associates to install an independent Election Commission, it is hoped that the upcoming elections will take place within an honest, just and fair environment. It goes without saying that the Pakistan Muslim League-Nawaz (PML-N) and other parties constantly trying to sabotage these accords will be punished on the Election Day by the "people power". Most of us are surprised with the role of some of our media and those ignorant people who are still suspecting Qadri and his associates in the electoral cleansing although he has publicly announced that neither he nor any of his family members would be taking part in the upcoming elections. My only reminder to these critics is that it only takes one honest, sincere and selfless individual like Qadri to lead a revolution of far-reaching consequences. History is witness to this fact—Quaid-e-Azam's movement for Pakistan, Ayatollah Khomeini's movement for a corruption-free Iran, Gandhi's movement to free India from the British rule, Mao Tse-tung's movement to liberate China and Fidel Castro's fight to throw American influence out of their country are just some examples of a one-man revolution.

The Islamabad bunker accord and the Lahore MQ Secretariat agreement have clearly drawn up the "mass line" which is the political, organizational and leadership method to defeat the corrupt politicians and the corrupt political practices in Pakistan as it did in China. The honest and sincere leaders of Pakistan must attribute their conquest of power to the faithful pursuit of effective "mass line" tactics; and an honest and timely "mass line" is the prerequisite for defeating the evil and corrupt politicians in Pakistan.

Who are the honest and sincere leaders in Pakistan today? The names of Imran Khan, General (Retd.) Pervez Musharraf, Tahir-ul Qadri and a few more will and have instantly popped up on the public screen. These leaders have clearly demonstrated their honesty and effectiveness, time and again, leaving a few unrelated odd instances. If the mass line in Pakistan is exposed to the corruption of the corrupt politicians through the competent documents and videos that are available in the archives and the honest leaders draw inspiration from the public and orient their political and organizational tactics to their responsiveness, the mass line tactics will destroy the corrupt political parties and their leaders.

A former senior official of the Election Commission of Pakistan, Kanwar Muhammad Dilshad, has stated to The Nation newspaper that the agreement between the government and Qadri would cleanse the electoral process of all corrupt practices and throw out of the elections 70 percent of the incumbent MPs who have been winning the past polls only because of their money and influence under the plutocratic system of government. This plutocracy is breathing its last, paving way to true democracy as the Election Commission of Pakistan quietly watches the implementation of the Islamabad bunker accord and the Lahore MQ Secretariat agreement before polls.

References

Published in The Kooza: February 03, 2013
Published in World News Network: February 7, 2013

Statements

ECP must allow Overseas Pakistanis to take part in General Elections

*IFES suggested the reservation of
some seats in Pakistan parliament
for overseas Pakistanis*

The Overseas Pakistanis Foundation (OPF) welcomes the decision made by the Election Commission of Pakistan (ECP) to give the right to vote in the general elections of Pakistan to about four million overseas Pakistanis living abroad across the world. On behalf of OPF and Friends of Pakistan in Canada we would like to extend our appreciation and thanks to Mr. Ishtiaq Ahmad Khan, ECP Secretary and other participants of the meeting who took a timely decision on a long overdue demand of Overseas Pakistanis to vote in the general elections.

Although ECP has crossed the bridge to allow "voting rights" to Overseas Pakistanis, they stopped short of two other crucial demands of Overseas Pakistanis i.e., to take part in the general Elections (by amending Article 63(1) of the constitution) and to reserve seats to Overseas Pakistanis in Pakistani parliament. In my article published in The Lahore Times on December 21, 2011, I strongly condemned the decision of ECP to disallow Overseas Pakistanis to take part in the elections under Article 63(1) and appealed that Overseas Pakistanis should not be deprived of their political and social rights as granted under the Constitution to the citizen of Pakistan.

The International Foundation for Electoral Systems (IFES) has also recommended that some parliamentary seats should be reserved for Overseas Pakistanis. Overseas Pakistanis represent over 20% of the total population of Pakistan and based on proportional representation around 65 seats can be allocated to Overseas Pakistanis in National parliament. The elections on these seats can be organized by applying same rules as for any other constituency except that the voting on these seats could take place outside Pakistan in

Pakistan High Commission offices, Embassies and Consulate offices across the world.

OPF which has its head office in Calgary, Canada and its executive members include Burhan Khan (Canada), Lord Nazir Ahmad (UK), Dr. Khalid Luqman Chaudhry (USA), Ali Abbas Hasanie (Canada), HE Javed Malik (UAE) and Zubair Nabi (Canada). OPF is an NGO whose objectives are to safeguard the rights of Dual Nationals in Pakistan and to provide a forum to Dual Nationals to participate in the affairs of Pakistan. OPF is deeply concerned over the exclusion of Dual National Pakistanis from taking part in the general elections and they have hired services of an attorney in Pakistan who is working with OPF to pursue this matter with the Government of Pakistan, the Supreme Court as well as with major political parties.

OPF makes a request to all political parties in Pakistan to present a Bill in the parliament to amend Article 63(1) of the constitution to allow dual nationals to participate in upcoming general elections.

OPF has sent a letter to ECP to look into the issues of Dual Nationals taking part in the elections and Pakistan allocating seats in the national parliament to Overseas Pakistanis. OPF has reiterated that Overseas Pakistan forms a significant part of Pakistan population and their contribution to the national treasury of Pakistan exceeds over 11 billion dollars a year.

References

Published in The Lahore Times: February 15, 2012

ECP grants overseas Pakistanis right to vote

The Executive Committee and the members of Overseas Pakistanis Forum (OPF) welcome the decision of the Election Commission of Pakistan (ECP) to grant the right to vote to Overseas Pakistanis in general elections of Pakistan. OPF would like to offer its assistance to ECP and other regulatory and governmental agencies in establishing the procedures to properly integrate this change in the political process of the country.

While OPF appreciates and commends on timely declaration for the right to vote in general elections, they are disappointed that ECP did not go far enough in their declaration to allow "Dual National Pakistani Citizens" to take part in general elections by amending Article 63(1) of the Constitution of Pakistan. We strongly demand that Article 63(1) be amended in the parliament to allow Dual National citizens to take part in elections similar to other citizens of Pakistan.

OPF would also like to appeal to political parties of Pakistan to join OPF in their demand to amend Article 63(1) of the constitution to allow Dual National Pakistani Citizens to take part in elections of Pakistan. OPF hopes and prays that all political parties will immediately move a Bill in the parliament amending Article 63(1) in order to allow Dual National citizens to take part in upcoming general elections.

On behalf of overseas Pakistanis, OPF is willing to participate in any meetings, discussions or proceedings organized by ECP, government agencies or political parties to speed up this process before upcoming elections.

On behalf of Overseas Pakistanis Foundation
Ali Abbas Hasanie, Secretary

References

Published in The Kooza February 16, 2012

Dual Nationality Bill in Pakistan is a step in right direction

The secretary of Overseas Pakistanis Forum (OPF), Ali Abbas Hasanie, made a statement that Dual Nationality Bill is a step in the right direction, as this Bill will recognize the full rights of Pakistanis with dual nationality. Mr. Hasanie reminded that in a press release issued by OPF on February 15, 2012, while welcoming the decision of Election Commission of Pakistan to grant the right of vote to overseas Pakistanis, OPF has demanded that Article 63(1)(C) be amended in the parliament to allow Dual National citizens to take part in elections similar to other citizens of Pakistan. He said that the decision of Government to amend the provision of Article 63 (1) (C) will give the rights to over four million overseas Pakistani voters to take part in the elections in Pakistan.

Mr. Hasanie has appealed to all political parties to support the Bill in the parliament because Pakistanis with dual nationality has the same allegiance to Pakistan and the people of Pakistan as any other Pakistani. He said that a "plural allegiance" does not take away or diminish the loyalty of a dual national Pakistani for Pakistan. He said this is a wrong concept that a dual national cannot be as loyal to Pakistan as someone with single nationality.

There are over 35 countries in the world including Pakistan, India, UK, USA, Canada, and France, which allow dual nationality to its citizens and most of them also allow these citizens to take part in their parliamentary and other elections. The dual nationality in modern times should be viewed as a means for people to globalize the freedom of rights to freely participate in political, social and economic well beings and thus help harmonize the relationship between the countries of their nationalities.

References

Published in The Lahore Times: July 11, 2012
Published in The Kooza
Published in World News Network

SC not doing justice if they don't recognize rights of dual national Pakistanis to be a parliamentarian

MONTREAL: The Overseas Pakistani Foundation (OPF) is concerned over the Supreme Court's decision on Tuesday to reserve the Judgment regarding the parliamentarians holding dual citizenship in the Senate, National and Provincial assemblies in Pakistan. OPF believes that the Supreme Court would not be doing justice as they recognize the right to vote to overseas Pakistanis in general elections but does not recognize their rights to be a parliamentarian.

The International Bill of Human Rights which consist of International Covenant of Civil and Political Rights (ICCPR) and Universal Declaration of Human Rights (UDHR) states:

(a) "Everyone has the right to take part in the government of his/her country . . . ." (Section 21(1) of ICCPR). Overseas Pakistanis with dual nationality claim Pakistan as his/her country; and Pakistan also considers them as its citizens since they hold National Identity Card, Pakistani Passport and the right to vote in the general elections. Therefore, they have the right to be a parliamentarian in Pakistan.

(b) "Everyone has the right to a nationality" Article 15 (1) of UDHR. A Pakistani who acquires the nationality of a foreign country where he resides without surrendering Pakistani citizenship is doing so as a "privilege" to enjoy the benefits of the resident country where he/she currently lives. This does not take away his/her allegiance to Pakistan.

OPF believes that in the definition of Article 63 (1) (c) the wordings "he ceases to be a citizen of Pakistan or acquire the citizenship of a foreign state" are narrowly interpreted by the courts as the intention of this clause ". . . . acquire the citizenship of a foreign state" is to acquire the citizenship of foreign state by giving up the citizenship of Pakistan, which is not the case with dual national Pakistanis. This is further confirmed by the declaration of Election Commission of Pakistan (ECP) that allowed the right of vote to dual national Pakistanis as they are considered to be citizens of Pakistan.

Mr. Burhan Khan, the chairman of OPF, believes that the honourable court is using an excessive power to disqualify parliamentarians with dual nationality; and feels it to be a total humiliation and against the dignity of human kind to call someone lesser of honest and custodian (Sadiq and Ameen).

In the end we strongly urge the honourable Supreme Court to consider overseas Pakistanis as part of Pakistani society who live outside as ambassadors of Pakistan and contribute heavily in the well-being, security and development of Pakistan, as citizens.

On behalf of Overseas Pakistanis Foundation
Ali Abbas Hasanie
Secretary

References

Published in The Lahore Times: September 20, 2012
Published in Kooza

Overseas Pakistanis sorrow over SC verdict

ISLAMABAD: The verdict of a three member bench of Supreme Court of Pakistan headed by Chief Justice Iftikhar Muhammad Chaudhry to seize membership of all parliamentarians that have dual nationality under article 63 (1) (C) of the constitution has been looked negatively by overseas Pakistanis who are of the view that the overseas Pakistanis are the second largest source of foreign exchange remittances to Pakistan after exports and over the last several years, the foreign exchange remittances have maintained a steady rising trend, with a recorded increase of 21.8% from $6.4 million in 2007-08 to $7.8 million during 2008-09. In 2009-10, Pakistani sent home $9.4 billion, the 11th largest in the world. By 2012, Pakistan increased its ranking to 10th in the world for remittances sent home at $13 billion per annum. The Overseas Pakistani Division (OPD) was created in September 2004 within the Ministry of Labour and Manpower. Since 2004, it has recognized the importance of overseas Pakistanis and their contribution to the economy. Together with Community Welfare Attaches (CWAs) and the Overseas Pakistanis Foundation (OPF), all three are improving the welfare of overseas Pakistanis. The division aims at providing better services to the overseas Pakistanis through improved facilities at airports, setting up suitable schemes in housing, education and health care. Its largest effort is facilitating the rehabilitation of returning overseas Pakistanis.

When contacted, Federal Minister for Overseas Pakistanis, Dr. Farooq Sattar said that the foreign remittances and investment in the country by overseas Pakistanis play a vital role in stabilizing the economy of Pakistan. He said the overseas Pakistanis are a great asset of the country that assist Pakistan and the government is taking several steps for their welfare. Farooq Sattar said that a stable Pakistan was in the best interest of the world adding that the people in Pakistan must be empowered to play an effective role.

Courtesy of "The Kooza" newspaper

**Supreme Court would not be doing justice as they recognize
the right to vote to Overseas Pakistanis in general elections but
do not recognize their rights to be a parliamentarian.**

Burhan Khan, the chairman of Overseas Pakistanis Foundation (OPF) Canada, believes that the honourable court is using an excessive power to disqualify parliamentarians with dual nationality; and feels it to be a total humiliation and against the dignity of human kind to call someone lesser of honest and custodian (Sadiq and Ameen). In the end we strongly urge the honourable Supreme Court to consider Overseas Pakistanis as part of Pakistan society who live outside as ambassadors of Pakistan and contribute heavily in the well-being, security and development of Pakistan, as citizens.

Ali Abbas Hasanie, Secretary Overseas Pakistanis Foundation Canada, while talking to The Kooza News Desk, was of the view that the SC verdict was not in accordance with the International Bill of Human Rights, which consist of International Covenant of Civil and Political Rights (ICCPR) and Universal Declaration of Human Rights (UDHR).

Universal Declaration of Human Rights (UDHR) states:

(a) "Everyone has the right to take part in the government of his/her country . . . ." Section 21(1) of ICCPR. Overseas Pakistanis with dual nationality claim Pakistan as his/her country; and Pakistan also considers them as their citizens since they hold National Identity Card, Pakistani Passport and the right to vote in the general elections. Therefore, they have the right to be a parliamentarian in Pakistan.

(b) "Everyone has the right to a nationality" Article 15 (1) of UDHR. A Pakistani who acquires the nationality of a foreign country where he resides without surrendering Pakistani citizenship is doing so as a "privilege" to enjoy the benefits of the resident country where he/she currently lives. This does not take away his/her allegiance to Pakistan.

OPF believes that in the definition of Article 63 (1) (c) the wordings "he ceases to be a citizen of Pakistan or acquire the citizenship of a foreign state" are narrowly interpreted by the courts as the intention of this clause ". . . . acquire the citizenship of a foreign state" is to acquire the citizenship of foreign state by giving up the citizenship of Pakistan, which is not the case with dual national Pakistanis. This is further confirmed by the declaration of Election Commission of Pakistan (ECP) that allowed the right of vote to dual national Pakistanis as they consider them the citizen of Pakistan.

References

Published in The Kooza: September 20, 2012

ECP must find mechanism to set up polling stations abroad for Overseas Pakistanis

The Election Commission of Pakistan's decision to advise over four million Pakistanis to go to Pakistan to cast their ballot is totally illogical and unpractical as these Pakistanis are not registered voters in any constituency in Pakistan due to their residency outside Pakistan. Also, the cost of fare and other inconvenience involved to travel to Pakistan just to cast their votes does not justify the trip to Pakistan. The reasons cited by ECP for its decision as legal hurdles and the unavailability of an adequate voting mechanism do not hold water since the Pakistani High Commissions and their consulate offices in every country of the world are exercising their executive powers in managing the affairs of Pakistanis without any legal hurdles or other inconveniences. So far, as the voting mechanism is concerned, it should not be any different than what they have been established inside the country. With the high-tech mechanism available in the world in every field for all kinds of checks and balances, it should not be difficult to set up polling stations in all major cities where overseas Pakistani live. Moreover, in most of the foreign countries, the Election Commission of that country would be willing to assist Pakistan in providing tools for polling such as ballot boxes, temporary polling stations and perhaps their staff to supervise the polling process. On behalf of overseas Pakistanis I would strongly urge Honorable Fakharuddin G. Ebrahim to please look into this very serious issue of overseas Pakistanis to exercise their right to vote in upcoming general elections

References

Published in The Lahore Times: September 29, 2012
Published in The Kooza

Expats may serve as polling officers, body of Canada-based Pakistanis tells ECP

MONTREAL: Praising Pakistan's Chief Election Commissioner Fakhruddin G Ebrahim, the Overseas Pakistani Forum has said Ebrahim can also count on overseas Pakistanis who will be willing to serve as polling officers in most cases without any remuneration or rewards.

Praising Ebrahim and his associates for making tireless efforts to hold the free and fair elections perhaps for the first time in the history of the country, Overseas Pakistani Forum Secretary Ali Abbas Hasanie noted in a statement that the setting of convenient polling stations and appointing impartial and honest polling officers are all in process and the Election Commission of Pakistan (ECP) is defining the qualifications and status of candidates for these vital positions.

"To set up the discipline for the polling stations and to declare the election results on a timely basis after the polls are still some challenges for ECP but we are confident that ECP will overcome these problems very soon," Hasanie said.

"Other rules such as the elections expenses, transparency of the polling process, role of media, gender disaggregated data, resolution of complains and above all the security and the fear of intimidation and coercion of voters, according to ECP, are all being addressed and will be resolved before the elections take place in the country," he noted.

Madam Louise Harel, Leader of the Official Opposition (Vision Montreal) City of Montreal, at the inauguration of a cricket tournament with Ali Abbas Hasanie at her side. Photo courtesy of office of Madam Harel, leader Vision Montreal party

Hasanie said the biggest fear of his organization at this point is that, while the elections under Ebrahim will be fair and clean, will the voters come out in larger number to defeat the corrupt, dishonest and incompetent politicians who have sadly made a mockery of democracy in Pakistan. "While Mr. Ibrahim will assure us of a free and fair election process, it is equally important that all of us must come out and vote to reject the failed and dishonest politicians known as the 'status-quo' parties who are in today's parliament and are responsible to bring the country on the brink of a failed state."

Hasanie appealed to everyone to consider the upcoming elections as a life and death situation for the country and elect the honest, capable and tested politicians who can bring the 'change' that is so badly needed in Pakistan. "Be aware of the politicians who have already been in power for two to three times and have failed miserably each time they were voted in power. Please don't forget next election is a test of people's power in Pakistan."

The secretary of the Overseas Pakistani Forum noted that the revised code of conduct, issued by ECP on November 8, along with the electoral reforms currently being debated with political parties and other stakeholders, is a clear indication ECP is serious and determined to hold unprecedented free and fair election in the country that is so desperately warranted.

Hasanie said the recent visit of Ebrahim to India to explore and analyze their electoral system to improve and strengthen the electoral system in Pakistan is a wise and bold step. "India is the largest democracy in the world while their elections are generally peaceful and fair considering that a large segment of their population is poor and not highly educated as compared to the Western countries."

The elections in a democratic society are a process that is made completely impartial and independent from all institutions, be it the military or the civil establishment or even the Supreme Court in exercising their *suo motu* power in the jurisdiction of the Election Commission, Hasanie said. No one but the chief election commissioner has the sole responsibility and power to organize and conduct elections once announced by the government and only he is answerable to the voters who place their blind trust in the Election Commission, he added.

Hasanie believed that the recent judgments of the Supreme Court in the Asghar Khan petition and other ongoing corruption cases in the Supreme Court along with the memories of public agitation after the 1977 election rigging should be a wake-up call to the voters to join hands and defeat the leaders who are involved in corruption but are still trying to fool people by their false statements and the deceitful acts.

References

Published in The Kooza: December 1, 2012

OPF requests nation to offer salute to CJP and OAS

MONTREAL, Dec. 27: The Secretary of Overseas Pakistani Forum (OPF), Ali Abbas Hasanie, has requested the nation to offer their salute to the Chief Justice of Pakistan, Justice Iftikhar Muhammad Chaudhry and the Chief of Army Staff General Ashfaq Parvez Kayani for extending their cooperation and support to the Election Commission of Pakistan in organizing free, fair and on-time general elections in Pakistan. Mr. Hasanie said that OPF is confident that free, fair and on-time election is a reality as promised by the Chief Election Commissioner Justice (Retd.) Fakhruddin G. Ebrahim.

On November 3, the Pakistan's National Judicial Committee, under the chairmanship of Chief Justice Iftikhar Muhammad Chaudhry, has agreed on relaxing of the restriction in supreme national interest on the involvement of the judiciary in the election process thereby providing services of an adequate number of judicial officers to ECP in the general elections.

On December 26, in the meeting of Chief Election Commissioner Justice (Retd.) Fakhruddin G. Ebrahim with the Chief of Army Staff (COAS) General Ashfaq Parvez Kayani.

General Kayani has extended his and army's complete support for the next general elections in Pakistan and pledged his full support for fair polls in the elections.

Now that two important national institutions Judiciary and Army have pledged their support to ECP, it is time for the Government to play their fair role in appointing the interim set-up with honest consultation from all parties that include political parties, Judiciary, Army and the Pakistan Election Commission, and declare the date of general elections according to the constitution of Pakistan. The Government must also realize that there are numerous challenges faced by the ECP before polling, therefore, enough time must be allowed to ECP to organize their tasks.

Mr. Hasanie has congratulated Dr. Tahir-ul Qadri for showing his courage and determination by demanding the Government to provide an environment with the consultation of all stakeholders, which is conducive to free and fair elections in Pakistan. The Government and the major political parties must realize that any attempt to undercut the fair election process will be challenged by the people of Pakistan under the leadership of Tahir-ul Qadri and many more who will join him for this very noble cause.

Mr. Hasanie has once again made a humble request to the voters to please show their strength by participating in large numbers and voting for honest, capable and tested leaders by breaking their loyalties to corrupt and incompetent political leaders and *biradaries*. Pakistan has never come so close to free and fair elections as this time and we must not lose this opportunity to bring the "Change" in Pakistan.

References

Published in The Kooza: December 28, 2012

Overseas Pakistanis have constitutional right to take part in country's affairs

Photo courtesy of The Kooza newspaper

The recent historical public meetings of Dr. Tahir-ul-Qadri have triggered heated and unnecessary debates over the role of overseas Pakistanis when it comes to affairs of Pakistan. These unwanted and unwarranted debates are a deliberate attempt to divert the attention of the public from the core issues at hand including the corrupt political system and the corrupt political practices of the corrupt and dishonest politicians who are hell-bent on seizing power at any cost in the upcoming elections in Pakistan. I am closely watching the interviews and talk-shows of Dr. Tahir-ul Qadri; and so far I am highly disappointed by the corrupt politicians and their supporters and how they have all launched a character assassination of a 'noble man' with a 'noble mission' by propagating irrelevant, useless and deceitful information just to dodge the core issue of 'Corruption' in the upcoming elections in Pakistan.

Let us first deal with the residency issue of overseas Pakistanis and their dual nationality. The Constitution of Pakistan does not impose any residential limitations whatsoever on the citizens of Pakistan whether they live within the boundaries of Pakistan or outside. Today, needless to say, the world is a global village and every free citizen on the earth has a right to live, to earn a living, to obtain education, to do business, to conduct research or to enjoy the various benefits as offered by their resident countries without disassociating themselves from their motherland. Some of the great revolutionary leaders of the world such as Ayatollah Khomeini, Jalaluddin Afghani, Mao Zedong, Mohandas Gandhi and Fidel Castro had all lived outside their home countries and upon the return to their homeland, they brought the greatest revolutions of their time, all for the right reasons.

A person who lives in Sindh for example, has every right to raise his voice against the injustices to his fellow citizens in Punjab; a person who is a resident in Khyber Pakhtunkhwa has every right to launch a protest against the brutality to his fellow citizens in Baluchistan. Similarly a Pakistani citizen who lives abroad has every right to launch a campaign in Pakistan against the corrupt political systems and corrupt politicians to safeguard the rights and interests of fellow citizens in his or her homeland—and no one has any right whatsoever to question his noble intentions on the grounds of his residency outside the country. Because the bottom line is that we are all Pakistani by heart, mind and soul regardless of where we may reside in the world, which is beside the point.

Some observers are raising a baseless issue over the oath taken by dual nationals to their resident countries at the time of assuming dual nationality. The Citizenship Act of Pakistan allows Pakistanis to take dual nationality of at least 16 countries without jeopardizing their Pakistani nationality. In my press release on September 21, 2012, I clarified that the allegiance given by dual national Pakistanis to their countries of residence for the reason of obtaining dual nationality, does not by any means compromise the relentless allegiance towards their homeland. The fact remains that it is the dual national Pakistanis who fight every day on the streets of foreign countries for Pakistan with their foreign governments if their governments or the people show any antagonism, unfairness, unfriendliness or conflict against Pakistan in any shape, way or form. It is these same Pakistanis who remit over $13 billion dollars annually to Pakistan, which is the second largest source of foreign exchange for Pakistan.

Apart from exploiting the residency issue, I also noted that these corrupt and dishonest politicians along with their supporters are constantly assassinating the character of Dr. Tahir-ul Qadri and trampling his sensible views—a man who has shaken the very dreams to capture the power by these corrupt politicians. These corrupt people along with some of our ignorant friends are blatantly accusing Dr. Qadri for derailing democracy, interrupting elections and overruling the authority of parliament and judiciary. I am shocked and amazed at how these people can misinterpret and undermine the current democracy in Pakistan that is nothing but a fraud and a game against the innocent people of Pakistan. The two major parties in Parliament along with their allies are simply making a mockery of democracy while suffocating the values as the people of Pakistan are sadly going through the worst and painful time in the history of Pakistan till date.

I am particularly disappointed and disillusioned with most of the people in our media who are unfortunately following the footsteps of our corrupt politicians while spending their time and energy in questioning Dr. Tahir-ul Qadri's honesty and truthfulness as well as his religious and spirituals beliefs plus his residency outside Pakistan along with the timing of his Mission. Towing the old and obsolete thinking, they are trying to link his noble Mission to some Western conspiracy, self fulfillment and a proxy war for the benefit of a third party which no one knows who that party is. We as a nation regrettably have lost our Faith and Trust in Honesty, Sincerity and Faithfulness by being submerged in a corrupt and unjust culture as our mind always steers towards the negative aspects of any issue.

Let me first clear the air by stating that I do not personally know Dr. Tahir-ul Qadri. Yes, I have listened to some of his speeches on Islam and his religious beliefs but no, I have never met him, never spoken to him in person or over the telephone and I have never attended any of his meetings or lectures. My only relation with him is that he is a man who has stood up against the "Corruption" which is the mother of all ills in Pakistan and I am strongly with him. As I have quoted in my last article in December 2012 that the democracy under the corrupt politicians is a fraud against the people of Pakistan. And I strongly commend and acknowledge Dr. Qadri on his wisdom, foresight and courage to take the Bull (which is corruption) by the horn without any fear or hesitation and with the support of millions of people to nib this *ahzab* (poison) in the bud.

For those people who are unfairly assassinating Dr. Qadri's character, I must add that from his background check, I firmly believe that he is 200% more honest than all of our politicians combined except for a few. His mission is noble, honest and free from all the political and non-political influences, be it from internal or external sources. His powerful and prevalent slogan "Save the State not the Politics" is timely and is the need of the day. His wisdom to correct the political system and to deter the corrupt politicians from capturing the power is "holy" and his "Long March" to Islamabad with millions of people to force the administration to reform the electoral system before the elections is truly justified and is what is finally needed today.

Dr. Qadri is the voice of millions of people in Pakistan who are crushed under the corrupt rule with no law and order, no jobs, no safety, no hope and without any future. He is a valiant warrior who has stood up to save the lives of people from the cruel forces who have killed thousands and thousands of people across our land in target killings, in sectarian killings, in ransom killings, and God-knows what other murders of innocent people. Dr. Qadri's mission is simple to take the support of masses and force the Government to set up an honest, just and independent body that can introduce the electoral reforms before the elections to pave the way for a free and fair election in Pakistan. He is not against the democracy at all nor is he is against the elections and he is not a candidate for any position in the interim government or even a candidate in the upcoming elections. He, and I am sure all of us, wants the honest and capable people to be elected in a free and fair election who can provide a good governance with a peaceful and prosperous living to our people.

Dr. Tahir-ul Qadri's respectful call for a "Long March" is the only peaceful way to force the reform of a corrupt electoral system in Pakistan thereby stopping the corrupt politicians to use unlawful means to capture power. It is our national duty to join this "Long March" and bring about the needed revolution in our country. We can do it!! We must do it!! China has done it, Iran has done it, Egypt has done it. They have all done it, and now the turn is ours, for our country by the people! We must be ready to provide the sacrifices to bring once and for all a sound and stabilized system which can place the true representatives of the people to power. The responsibility lies in each of our hands to morally do the right and needful action.

References

Published in The Kooza: January 16, 2013

Press Releases

Government must fulfill its reponsibility by providing safety and security to its citizens

Government must fulfill its responsibility to provide safety to lives and security to properties and investments of its citizen

Supreme court judgement must be respected to avoid anarchy in the country; parliament has no role in the court rooms of the nation

Political parties must refrain from taking advantage of the current crises; government must resign and call general elections

Overseas Pakistanis are very much disturbed about the current crises in Pakistan which have taken hundreds of innocent lives in target killings and collateral damages and have destroyed the properties and investments of citizens and made the lives of hundreds and thousands of people miserable due to shortage of electricity, food and other necessities of daily lives.

Overseas Pakistanis Forum (OPF) strongly condemns the insensitivity of the government in ignoring the sufferings of people and demands that the government of Pakistan must fulfill its responsibilities to provide safety to the lives and security to properties and investments of its citizens.

OPF believes that the Supreme Court of Pakistan is playing its fair and constitutional role in identifying and targeting the corrupt and cruel people; and by penalizing the leaders who are responsible to bring the country to its present chaotic state. OPF reminds political leaders, government and its bureaucrats that the judgments of Supreme Court must be respected to avoid anarchy. The government and political leaders must stop challenging the authority of judiciary as this may ultimately lead to the suspension of parliament and interruption of democratic system in order to salvage the security of Pakistan. This will be a sad day for the democracy in Pakistan and no one but the politicians will be responsible for such a grave outcome. OPF firmly believes that parliament can legislate the laws but has no role to play in the courtrooms of the nation and in the process of justice. Those who are committing crimes and are being penalized cannot take justice in their own hands to overrule the judgment of the court in the name of democracy.

OPF is very closely monitoring the situation in Pakistan; we have noticed that a few political leaders are taking advantage of the current crises and playing politics with the lives, properties and well being of the people by throwing fuel on fire to make political gains. These political games at the cost of human suffering must immediately be stopped. Considering the present critical situation in Pakistan, parties in government and in opposition must resign their seats in parliament and call immediate elections to avoid further deterioration in law and order situation in the country.

OPF and its members are willing to offer their services to bring the situation in Pakistan to normal, which is a pre-requisite for any free and fair elections.

On behalf of Overseas Pakistanis Forum

Ali Abbas Hasanie, Secretary

References

Published in The Lahore Times on June 9, 2012

Fakhruddin Ebrahim and his associates praised by OPF

MONTREAL: The Secretary of Overseas Pakistani Forum (OPF), Ali Abbas Hasanie, praised Honorable Fakhruddin G. Ebrahim, Chairman of Pakistan Elections Commission, and his associates for making tireless efforts to organize the free and fair elections perhaps for the first time in the history of Pakistan. He noted that the revised code of conduct, issued by ECP on November 8, 2012 along with the electoral reforms, which are currently being debated with political parties and other stakeholders, is a clear indication that ECP is serious and determined to deliver unprecedented free and fair election in the country that is so desperately warranted.

The recent visit of Mr. Ebrahim to India to explore and analyze their electoral system in order to improve and strengthen our own electoral system in Pakistan is a wise and bold step. India is the largest democracy in the world while their elections are generally peaceful and fair considering that a large segment of their population is poor and not highly educated as compared to the Western countries.

The elections in a democratic society are a process that is made completely impartial and independent from all institutions be it the military or the civil establishment or even the Supreme Courts in exercising their *suo motu* power in the jurisdiction of Elections Commission. No one but the Chief Election Commissioner has the sole responsibility and power to organize and conduct elections (once the elections are announced by the government) and only he is answerable to the voters who place their blind trust in the election commission.

Mr. Hasanie believes that the recent judgments of the SC in the Asghar Khan Petition and other ongoing corruption cases including NRO in the SC along with the memories of public agitation which aroused after the 1977 election bungling should be a "wake-up call" to the voters to join hands and defeat those leaders who are involved in these corruptions but are still trying to fool people by their false statements and the deceitful acts.

Mr. Hasanie noted that there is a serious debate in the country to dissolve the parliament and appoint the interim government before the elections, which in his opinion should have no bearing on the upcoming elections if the care-taking government stays within their mandate. The "Chief Boss" for the elections in any country is the Chairman of Election Commission and all other institutions including the current establishment, the interim government, Judiciary, political parties and the voters, directly report to the ECP on election issues. No one is allowed to interfere or cross the lines of the rules as set by the Elections Commission. The role of the interim government is to maintain the law and order while assisting the ECP in the administrative matters such as providing security and assisting in setting up polling booths etc.

One of the major concerns of the ECP has always been the electoral list which Mr. Tariq Malik, the chairman of NADRA, is already on record for testifying that the current list is accurate and complete. However, Mr. Ebrahim is still appealing to voters to obtain their NICs before the elections and verify their names in the electoral list, a process that has never happened very thoroughly in the past. The establishment of electoral constituencies is also an issue that is being looked into in the light of the recent directives from the SC.

The setting of convenient polling stations and appointing impartial and honest polling officers are all in process, and the ECP is defining the qualifications and status of candidates for these vital positions. Mr. Hasanie believes that Mr. Ebrahim can also count on overseas Pakistanis who will be willing to serve as polling officers in most cases without any remuneration or rewards. To set up the discipline for the polling stations and to declare the election results on a timely basis after the polls is still a challenge for ECP but we are confident that ECP will overcome these problems very soon. Other rules such as the elections expenses, transparency of the polling process, role of media, gender dis-aggregated data, resolution of complaints and above all the security and the fear of intimidation and coercion of voters, according to ECP, are all being addressed and will be resolved before the elections take place in the country.

OPF's biggest fear at this point is that, while the elections under Mr. Fukhruddin G. Ebrahim will be fair and clean, will the voters come out in larger number to defeat the corrupt, dishonest and incompetent politicians who have sadly made a mockery of democracy in Pakistan. While Mr. Ibrahim will assure us of a free and fair election process, it is equally important that all of us must come out and vote to reject the failed and dishonest politicians known as the *status quo* parties who are in today's parliament and are responsible to bring the country on the brink of a failed state.

Mr. Hasanie is appealing to everyone to please consider the upcoming elections as a life and death situation for the country and elect honest, capable and tested politicians who can bring the 'Change' that is so badly needed in Pakistan. Be aware of the politicians who have already been in power for two to three times and have failed miserably each time they were voted in power. Please don't forget next election is a test of people's power in Pakistan.

References

Published in The Lahore Times on December 1, 2012

Criticism of Qadri by Pakistani politicians, media disappoints OPF

MONTREAL: The Overseas Pakistanis Forum (OPF) has expressed its disappointment over what it called the treatment of Dr. Tahir-ul Qadri as a second-class citizen by some Pakistani political leaders and media on the ground of holding dual nationality.

In a statement issued here on Wednesday, Ali Abbas Hasanie, OPF secretary, said that while the Supreme Court followed its usual course of action in deciding the application of law to Dr. Qadri's petition, a number of political leaders and some media persons were criticizing Dr. Qadri's efforts to regularize the formation of the Election Commission of Pakistan (ECP).

Hasanie said the dual national Pakistanis are not second class citizens and they have constitutional rights to challenge the formation of the ECP, which if proven unconstitutional by the court after the elections might jeopardize the results of the election process in Pakistan.

The OPF secretary said that over 4.3 million Pakistanis living outside Pakistan have their *locus standi* against what he called the corrupt politicians and the corrupt electoral process as they see their homeland gradually sinking and reaching to a point of a failed state.

"Is this not enough reason for the likes of Dr. Qadri to return back to Pakistan and save Pakistan from the hostile takeover by the corrupt politicians in upcoming elections? I am not a constitutional lawyer and I cannot comment on the application of Article 184(3) and *quo warranto* but I can assure you that the people of Pakistan have high hopes over the role of apex court in Pakistan to ensure free, fair, honest and just elections. The voters are confident that our apex court will definitely pull a *suo motu* action when they have a reason to believe that Election Commission and/or interim prime minister are not exercising their power in a free, fair, honest and just manner," he stated.

Hasanie reiterated that dual national Pakistanis are as much Pakistanis as any other Pakistani living inside Pakistan. He said the dual national Pakistanis have a constitutional right to take part in the affairs of Pakistan and to fully participate in Pakistani elections. "No one needs to suspect the loyalty of dual national Pakistanis as they can leave their country of residence to come back to Pakistan by giving up their dual nationality on a few days notice. We must understand that the oath for the loyalty of a resident country outside Pakistan is by design but the loyalty to our homeland is by our choice and faith," he argued.

As Salman Akram Raja, a senior lawyer, said the oath of allegiance to any country is there to be loyal to the constitution and the state in the law making (parliamentarians only) and in abiding by the laws of the land (which is not wrong), the OPF secretary said. But if the question of allegiance to Pakistan against a foreign country ever comes, he said, Pakistanis would be on the side of Pakistan and not on the side of a foreign country where they live.

"On behalf of OPF, I would like to assure Dr. Qadri and his associates that we are all with you for your efforts for justice in Pakistan and free and fair elections to bring a change in government for the survival and the betterment of Pakistan," he concluded.

References

Published in The Kooza: February 13, 2013

Key Events in Pakistan

Pakistan—Key events in chronological order

December 30, 1906	All India Muslim League gets formed
1930	Allama Mohammad Iqbal calls for an autonomous state for Muslims
June 1947	National leaders of British India including Jawaharlal Nehru and Abul Kalam Azad representing the Congress, Muhammad Ali Jinnah representing All India Muslim League, Master Tara Singh representing Sikhs agree to terms with British rulers of transfer of power and independence.
October 27, 1947	Indian air troops land in Kashmkir as Maharaja Hari Singh declares accession of Jammu and Kashmir to India
September 11, 1948	Quaid-e-Azam Muhammed Ali Jinnah passed away while Pakistan remains in its infancy and no leadership developed in Pakistan.
February 25, 1948	Urdu is declared as the national language of Pakistan
March 12, 1949	Constituent assembly of Pakistan adopts Objective Resolution as a guide for constitution—Pakistan declares itself as Islamic state
July 26, 1949	Pakistan and India agree on cease fire line in Jammu and Kashmir
1949	Souviet Union invites Liaqat Ali Khan Prime Minister to USSR
October 1, 1949	People Republic of China founded
January 4, 1950	Government of Pakistan recognizes Peoples Republic of China
April 8, 1950	Liaqat-Nehru agreement signed in New Delhi on measures to deal with major Inter-Dominion problems
October 16, 1951	Quaid-e-Millat Liaqat Ali Khan PM was assassinated under highly controversial circumstances in both internal and external politics in Rawalpindi.
March 6, 1953	Disturbance arises against Ahmadis and government promulgated Martial law in Punjab.
April 17, 1953	Malik Ghulam Mohammad, Governor General (GG), dissolves the civilian government of Khwaja

	Nazimuddin, Prime Minister (PM) over the dispute of power sharing between GG and PM.
August 7, 1954	Government approves National Anthem written by Abdul Aser Hafeez Jullindhari and composed by Ahmad Chagla
September 21, 1954	Constituent assembly passes resolution in favour of Urdu and Bengali as national languages of Pakistan
August 6, 1955	Mohammad Ali Bogra PM was forced to resign by Iskandar Mirza over the internal dispute of power sharing and regional disparity
August 7, 1955	Chaudhry Mohammad Ali gets elected as Prime Minister, after Mohammad Ali Bogra resigns
October 6, 1955	Malik Ghulam Mohammad resigns as Governor General and Major General Iskander Mirza becomes Governor General
March 23, 1956	First ever Constitution of Pakistan promulgated, Major General Iskandar Mirza becomes first President
September 12, 1956	Chaudhry Mohammad Ali PM was forced to resign under political pressure from Major General Iskander Mirza over internal politics.
October 17, 1957	Husayn Shaheed Sahrwardy PM was forced to resign by Iskandar Mirza President over the control of power 1957 Governor raj imposed in West Pakistan
December 16, 1957	Malik Feroz Khan Noon sworn in as 7th Prime Minister
December 17, 1957	Iskandar Mirza President forced Ibrahim Ismail Chundrigar PM to resign.
June 25, 1958	President rule is proclaimed in East Pakistan
October 7, 1958	Malik Feroz Khan Noon PM was sacked by President Iskandar Mirza due to military pressure of General Ayub Khan C-in-C.
October 7, 1958	Martial Law is declared throughout the country, General Mohammad Ayub Khan becomes the chief Martial Law Administrator.
November 2, 1958	President Iskander Mirza was forced to resign by the military and sent into exile to London U.K.
March 3, 1958	Martial Law authority enforces PRODA to disqualify veteran politician under Elective Bodies Disqualification Order (EBDO)
March 1959	One Unit was imposed in Pakistan and provinces dissolved

March 23, 1962	New constitution promulgated by Ayub Khan regime, Pakistan transpires from a parliamentary government to presidential form of government.
June 8, 1962	New assembly gets elected under 1962 constitution, General Mohammad Ayub Khan took oath as first president of Pakistan under 1962 constitution
September 6, 1965	India attacks Pakistan without the declaration of War over Kashmir issue
September 23, 1965	India and Pakistan signs cease-fire
January 10, 1966	Tashkent Declaration signed between India and Pakistan as mediated by the USSR
February 12, 1966	Sheikh Mujibur Rehman Chief of Awami League announces his party's six points in Karachi for upcoming elections in Pakistan
January 6, 1968	Agartala conspiracy case for secession of East Pakistan was unearthed. 28 involved persons get arrested alongwith Mujibur Rehman.
November 7, 1968	Student demonstration starts through the country leading to the resignation of President Ayub Khan.
February 1969	President Ayub Khan requests Nawabzada Nasrullah Khan to call a meeting of all opposition leaders in Pakistan to find the solution to law and order in the country due to political and student unrest
March 25, 1969	President, Ayub Khan resigns and hands over the power to General Mohammad Yahya Khan who dissolved assemblies and proclaimed Martial law
December 1, 1969	303 government officers and bureaucrats involved in corruption were suspended
July 1, 1970	One Unit was dissolved, and provinces got restored.
December 7, 1970	Awami League emerged as a Winner in the general elections, Pakistan People party refused to accept the election results.
March 26, 1971	Pakistan army launches operation in East Pakistan
November 22, 1971	India launches full scale attack on East Pakistan
December 16, 1971	Dhakka falls in the hands of Indian Army and Bangladesh comes into being
December 20, 1971	General Yahya Khan hands over power to Zulfiqar Ali Bhutto who took over as President and Chief Martial Administrator
January 8, 1972	Sheikh Mujibur Rehman, arrested for breaking East Pakistan was released unconditionally

January 30, 1972	Zulfiqar Bhutto withdraws Pakistan from Commonwealth, SEATO and CENTO over the acceptance of Bangladesh by Commonwealth.
April 10, 1972	Zulfiqar Ali Bhutto gets elected President by the National assembly.
July 2, 1972	Simla agreement signed between Pakistan and India, over the war in East Pakistan
1972	Karachi Labour Unrest starts
April 10, 1973	1973 Constitution of Pakistan enacted by the National assembly
August 11, 1973	Zulfiqar Ali Bhutto becomes Prime Minister and Chaudhri Fazal Elahi becomes President
August 28, 1973	Prisoners of war return to Pakistan, Accord signed in New Delhi
February 21, 1974	Pakistan recognizes Bangladesh
February 22, 1974	Islamic conference starts in Lahore—22 heads of Muslim states participated.
September 7, 1974	Pakistan National assembly passed a law declaring the members of Ahmadi movement as non-muslim.
March 1, 1976	General Mohammad Ziaul Haq becomes Chief of Army Staff.
March 7, 1977	General elections held in Pakistan, Pakistan People's party wins 155 seats out of 200. Opposition parties rejected the results of elections and staged protest which caused major unrest in the country.
July 5, 1977	General Ziaul Haq dissolves the government and enforces Martial law, suspends constitution and banns all political activities.
September 17, 1977	Zulfiqar Ali Bhutto, prime minister, was arrested under Martial law orders
March 18, 1978	Lahore High Court awarded death sentence to Zulfiqar Ali Bhutto alongwith four others
September 16, 1978	Altaf Hussain forms All Pakistan Muhajir Students Organization
September 16, 1978	General Ziaul Haq sworn in as President
1979	Hudood Ordinance gets enacted
February 6, 1979	Supreme court upholds Bhutto's conviction in Mohammad Ahmad Khan murder case
April 4, 1979	Zulfiqar Ali Bhutto was hanged in Rawalpindi jail
October 16, 1979	Ziaul Haq puts off Polls indefinitely; political parties dissolved, press censorship imposed

May 26, 1980	Establishment of Federal Shariat Court is announced
June 21, 1980	Government starts collecting Zakat from citizens
February 9, 1984	Government imposes ban on all students unions
April 27, 1984	Ban was imposed on the use of Islamic nomenclatures by Ahmadis
December 19, 1984	General Ziaul Haq holds Presidential referendum
Fbruary 25, 1985	Party less national general elections held
1985	Nawaz Sharif gets appointed as Chief Minister of Punjab by Ziaul Huq's military regime
April 15, 1985	Death of Bushra Zaidi a university student engenders series of roits
October 16, 1985	National assembly adopts Eighth Amendment Bill, changing Pakistani's system of Government from parliamentary democratic republic to semi-predential system.
December 16, 1985	Martial law was lifted and 1973 Constitution gets amended before adoption.
April 10, 1986	Benazir Bhutto returns to homeland from exile after 7 years
April 8, 1988	Army ammunition blows up in Ojheri Campt Rawalpindi, 100 people died
June 15, 1988	President Ziaul Haq promulgated Shariat Ordinance making Shariat Supreme Law of the land
May 29, 1988	President, General Ziaul Haque dissolves National assemblies and the government of Prime Minister Muhammad Khan Jonejo.
August 17, 1988	President General Ziaul Haq was killed in a plane crash near Bahawalnagar
August 1988	General Aslam Beg announces general elections in the country.
October 6, 1988	Eight political parties forms Islamic Jamhuri Ittihad (IJI) with the help of establishment
December 2, 1988	Benazir Bhutto sworn in as first women Prime Minister of Pakistan
October 1, 1989	Pakistan re-joins Commonwealth
November 1, 1989	No-confidence move against Prime Minister Benazir Bhutto fails
August 6, 1990	President Ghulam Ishaq Khan dissolved National assembly and dismissed Benazir Bhutto government on the charges of corruption

October 24, 1990	General elections took place, IJI got 104 seat, PDA won 45 seats
November 6, 1990	Nawaz Sharif becomes Prime Minister after leading Islamic democratic Alliance organized by establishment
November 8, 1990	Nawaz Sharif de—nationalizes major industries after launching privatization and economic liberation
1991	Nawaz Sharif contends with Chief of Army staff general Mirza Aslam Beg over the gulf War (Operation Desert Storm)
1991	General Aslam Beg gets replaced as Cheif of Army staff by Nawaz Sharif PM and general Asif Nawaz gets appointed as cheif of army staff.
May 16, 1991	National assembly adopted Shariat Bill (Shariat Ordinance of June 15, 1988)
June 19, 1992	Military operation starts in Sindh
1992	Nawaz Sharif quarreled with COAC General Asif Nawaz on operation in Sindh
April 18, 1993	President Ghulam Ishaq Khan dissolves National assembly and dissolves Nawaz Sharif government on the charges of corruption
January, 1993	General Asif Nawaz Chief of Army dies of heart attack.
January 1993	Dispute arises between Nawaz Sharif PM and Ghulam Ishaq Khan President over the appointment of new COAS—Ghulam Ishaq Khan appoints General Wahid Kakar as new COAS under the power given by the constitution
May 1993	Nawaz Sharif was dismissed as Prime Minister and National assembly gets dissolved by the President on the charges of corruption
May 26, 1993	Supreme Court restored National Assembly and reinstated Prime Minister Nawaz Sharif
July 18, 1993	President Ghulam Ishaq Khan and Prime Minister Nawaz Sharif resign their offices with the efforts of Army chiefs
October 6, 1993	General elections took place—Pakistan Peoples party win 86 seats and PML-N wins 72 seats; Benazir Bhutto gets elected as Prime Minister
November 13, 1993	Farooq Lagari gets elected eight President of Pakistan

December 6, 1995	Lahore High Court dismisses appeal against Major General Zaheerul Islam Abbasi in Khilafat conspiracy case
1995	General Jehangir Karamat thwarting the conspiracy against PM Benazir Bhutto—Benazir appoints General Jehangir Karamat as chief of army staff and chairman of joint staff committee.
September 20, 1996	Mir Murtaza Bhutto a political leader and son of Z.A. Bhutto was assinated in Karachi during Bhazir Bhutto's government.
November 5, 1996	President Farooq Lagari dissolved National assembly and sacked Prime Minister Benazir Bhutto government on charges of corruption.
February 3, 1997	Nation goes to Polls—PML-N wins 135 seats; Nawaz Sharif sworn in as Prime Minister
February 17, 1997	Nawaz Sharif gets 2/3 majority in parliameant and gets appointed as Prime Minister
April 2, 1997	13th Amendment was passed stripping President of all its power.
October 1997	14th Amendment "Horse Trading and Lotacracy" was passed by Nawaz Sharif parliament which banned the practice of switching sides (parties) by members of parliament
October	Chief Justice rejected 14th amendment as unconstitutional
November 1997	Nawaz Sharif accused President Lagari to undermine his government
November 1997	Nawaz Sharif developed severe tussel with judiciary (Chief Justice Sajjad Shah) over the appointment of judges to supreme court and undermining his government. Sajjad Shah, CJ, was lone dissident in the case to restore Nawaz Sharif government in May 1993.
November 1997	Nawaz Sharif was charged with contempt of court by Supreme Court
November 1997	Parliament amended Pakistan's contempt of court law giving PM Nawaz Sharif an option to appeal which suspends the conviction while appeal is being heard
November 1997	Amendment to contempt of court law by Nawaz Sharif drived the country into Constitutional crises; President Farooq Lagari refuses to sign the amendment.

November 1997	Nawaz Sharif intended to impeach President Farooq Lagari on his refusal to sign the amendment passed by the parliament regarding the appeal to contempt of court judgement by SC
November 1997	The proceeding on the impeachment of President Lagari was halted when Army stepped in mediate between Prime Minister and President.
November 1997	A full bench of 15 judges took up the petition challenging the appointment of Sajjad Ali Shah as Chief Justice. CJ cancelled this hearing on illegal ground.
November 1997	Chief Justice Sajjad Ali Shah upheld the decision of President on the dismissal of Benazir Bhutto government
November 1997	Shahbaz Sharif and justice (Retd.) Rafique Tarar (Nawaz Sharif's party senator) approached the judges of Baluchistan bench to form a lobby with like minded judges of Baluchistan and NWFP to start proceeding against Chief Justice Sajjad Ali Shah on his appointment as CJ
November 1997	Nawaz Sharif supporters stormed supreme court during court proceedings of CJ Sajjad Ali Shah on contempt charges on Nawaz Sharif and a major scuffle ensued with judiciary Supreme court called army for protection of SC
November 1997	Nawaz Sharif criticized CJ decision as "illegal and unconstitutional" and further stated that CJ had created a situation that was both unfortunate and undemocratic.
November 1997	Nawaz Sharif submits his apology, Chief justice adjourns hearing till he reviews video tape of news conference of Nawaz Sharif, which contains criticism of SC
1997	Nawaz Sharif established special courts in contravention of CJ advise to benefit his allies and supporters eventually proved to be a humiliating blot on the face of justice system of Pakistan
December 2, 1997	CJ Sajjad Ali Shah was forced to resign by Nawaz Sharif
December 2, 1997	President Farooq Lagari was forced to resing by Nawaz Sharif
January 1, 1998	Rafique Tarar sworn in as President

May 28, 1998	Pakistan conducts Nuclear test in Chagai hills in Baluchistan
1998	After the Nuclear test, PM Nawaz Sharif chaired the Defence Committee of the Cabinet (DCC) session with the chairman and chief of armed forces to overview the situation with India
1998	General Jehangir Karamat stressed the re-creation of National Security Council (NSC) instead of DCC based on a team of civil-military experts to seek resolution in civil military issues.
May 29, 1998	State Bank of Pakistan bans the opening of new foreign exchange accounts and suspends withdrawals of foreign exchange
June 1, 1998	UN Security Coluncil denies Nuclear power status to India and Pakistan
October 6, 1998	Nawaz Sharif dismissed General Jehangir Karamat and signed his relieving papers which surprised many as the dismissal of four-star General never happened in the past
October 6, 1998	General Pervez Musharraf was appointed at Chief of Army staff
October 7, 1998	General Jehangir Karamat resigned due to conflict with PM Nawaz Sharif
1999	Nawaz Sharif dismisses Admiral Fasih Bukhari and promotes General Pervez Musharraf to Chairman of Joint Staff committee.
January 1999	Nawaz Sharif forced the Jang Group to suspend its publication over allegations of widespread corrupt practices by Sharif family and close associates
February 21, 1999	Lahore Declaration was signed by Nawaz Sharif PM and A.B. Vajpayee PM India—no mention of Kashmir; Army became unhappy
April 15, 1999	Pakistan conducts test of Nuclear capable short range ballistic missile—Shaheen
May-July 1999	Armed conflict broke out between Pakistan and India over Kashmir issue along line of Control in the district of Kargil, Kashmir
July 26, 1999	Kargil war ends between India and Pakistan
October 12, 1999	Military Generals thrown out Nawaz Sharif from power and placed him under house arrest after his attempt to sack General Pervez Musharraf and to

	appoint General Ziauddin Butt as chief of armed forces and chairman of joint staff committee
October 17, 1999	Nawaz Sharif was house arrest on hijacking of plane and terrorism charges.
1999	Pakistan was suspended from Commonwealth over Martial Law in October 1999.
April 6, 2000	Nawaz Sharif was sentenced to life imprisment on charges of high jacking of a plane and terrorism
May 13, 2000	Supreme Court (Iftikha Chaudhry—Chief Justice) validated October 1999 coup and General Pervez Musharraf was given three years t o bring democratic government
August 14, 2000	Pervez Musharraf introduced local government system
December 10, 2000	Pervez Musharraf pardoned all cases against Nawaz Sharif and Shahbaz Sharif alongwith his family before they went into Exile in Saudi Arabia.
June 20, 2001	Pervez Musharraf assumed office of President while remaining Chief of army Staff.
July 15, 2001	Agra summit starts in Agra India—President Musharraf and Prime Minister Vajpayee holds talks over long outstanding issues between Pakistan and India
August 14, 2001	New local government gets installed after local body elections
September 11, 2001	World Trade center in New York USA got attacked and destroyed
September 16, 2001	US Secretary of State Powell told President of Pakistan and President of Pakistan agreed to support the US anti-terrorism campaign and fight
April 30, 2002	Pervez Musharraf wins in a Referendum
August 24, 2002	Pervez Musharraf issues Legal Frame Work Order (LFO) 2002
October 10, 2002	General elections held in the country—Pakistan Muslim League-Quaid-e-Azam (PML-Q) holds most seats in the election—Mir Zafrullah Jamali sworns in as Prime Minister
February 24, 2003	Senate elections held—PML-Q holds majority.
January 1, 2004	Pervez Musharraf wins vote of confidence in Senate, National and Provincial assemblies
May 22, 2004	Pakistan got re-admitted to Commonwealth after it was suspended in 1999 over Martial Law
July 14, 2005	NWFP assembly passes HASBA Bill

October 8, 2005	A devastating earthquake hits Kashmir and Khyber Pakhtunkhwa and kills over eighty thousand people.
May 14, 2006	Charter of Democracy (COD) got signed between Nawaz Sharif and Benazir Bhutto in London U.K.
August 26, 2006	Akbar Bugti got killed in military confrontation
March 9, 2007	Pervez Musharraf dismisses Chief Justice Iftikhar Chaudhry on alleged charges.
July 20, 2007	Iftikhar Chaudhry gets restored as Chief Justice.
October 18, 2007	Benazir Bhutto returns to Pakistan after exile of 8 years
November 3, 2007	Pervez Musharraf imposes Emergency and most of the judges of Supreme Court got ousted
2007	Pakistan got thrown out of Commonwealth for imposing Emergency rule till the restoration of democracy
November 25, 2007	Nawaz Sharif returns to Pakistan after 7 years in exile
December 27, 2007	Benazir Bhutto gets assassinated in Rawalpindi after public meeting.
January 2, 2008	New elections were called for February 18, 2008.
February 18, 2008	General elections held—PPP (124), PML-N (91), PML-Q (54) and ANP (13), PPP forms the government with the alliance of PML-N and ANP
August 18, 2008	Pervez Musharraf steps down as President. 1973 Constitution gets amended to cut down the power of President to dissolve assembly.
September 6, 2008	Asif Zardari got elected as President
February 16, 2009	Government announces a truce with Taliban accepting a system of Islamic law in Swat Valley conceding the area as Taliban territory
May 2009	Taliban rejected the writ of the government
May 23-July 15, 2009	Army launches operation "Rah-e—Rast" and cleared Swat valley of Taliban elements. It is regarded as one of the most successful insurgency operation in modern age
April 2010	Parlaiment approves package of wide ranging constitutional reforms. Measures include transferring of key power from the office of President to Prime Minster.
2010	Rise in targeted sectarian and political killings, bombing takes place in commercial hub of Karachi
January-March 2011	A campaign to reform Pakistan's blashemy law leads to the killing of two prominent supporters of reform,

	Punjab governor Salman Taseer (January 2011) and Minorities minister Shahab Bhatti (March 2011).
April 2011	Founder of Al-Qaeda Osama bin Laden got killed by American special forces in Abbottabad, Pakistan.
April 2011	Memogate scandal—government of PPP comes under pressure over the leaked memo alleging senior officers in government seeking US aid against the military coup after killing of Osama bin Laden
May 21, 2011	Chief justice Chaudhry Iftikahr Ahmad consents to acquit Nawaz Sharif from plane high jacking case.
November 2011	Pakistan shuts down NATO supply route after a NATO attack on military out posts killing 25 Pakistan soldiers
December 2011	Pakistan boycotts the BAUN conference of Afghanistan in protest of NATO attack on border check points in Pakistan
2011	US troops leaves Shams air base in Baluchistan in the wake of November NATO attack
2012	Amid growing tense between military and government over Memogate scandal—Army chief general Pervez Kiyani warns "unpredicrtable consequences" after PM Raza Gilani criticizes army leaders and sacks two top defence officials.
2012	US senate cuts 33 million dollars in aid to Pakistan over the jailing of Pakistan, doctor Shakil Afridi who helped the CIA find Osama bin Laden. Dr. Afridi was tried for treason under a tribunal justice system for running a false vaccination program to gather information for the US intelligence.
June 2012	Supreme court convicts PM Raza Gilani in contempt of court and disqualifies him from holding office of PM after he declines to appeal against President Asif Zardari corruption case
2012	Raja Pervez Ashraf, former Water and Power minister charged in corruption, takes over the office of Prime Minister.
July 2012	Pakistan agrees to open NATO supplies route after US apologises for killing Pakistani soldiers
September 2012	Muslim cleric Khalid Chishti got arrested on suspicion of planting pages of holy Quran amongst the burnt papers in the bag of Christian girl in November

2012	Pakistan security forces stops Imran Khan's major rally against US drone attack in the town Tank
2012	Taliban gunman seriously injured 14 years old girl Malala Yousafza who campaigned for girls' rights. She got targeted in Swat valley for promoting secularism
November 2012	Taliban suicide bomber kills at least 23 people at a shia Muslim procession in Rawalpindi
2012	Blast in shia mosque in Karachi kills at least two people
2012	Bomb blast in Quetta leaves five dead in the holy month of Ramadhan
December 23, 2012	Dr. Tahir-ul Qadri popular cleric and head of Tehreek-e-Pakistan and anti corruption campaigner addresses political gathering at Minar-e-Pakistan to protest against corruption and demanded electoral reforms before upcoming elections
January 2013	Dr. Tahir-ul Qadri leads a nationwide long March to Islamabad and holds four-day rally in Islamabad demanding the electoral reforms, the resignation of the government and the dissolution of assembly
January 2013	Supreme court orders arrest of Prime Minister Raja Pervez Ashraf over the corruption allegation as Water and Power minister
2013	Bomb blasts in Quetta killing at least 122 shia Muslim—Sunni extremist group Lashkar-e-Jhangvi claims responsibility for the blast
2013—	Federal government sacks Chief minister of Baluchistan over bomb blast in Quetta
January 2013	After four day protest in the capital, the government agrees to dissolve parliament early and agreed to implement most of Dr. Qadri's demands including consultation over the formation of caretaker government ahead of elections
2013	Bomb attacks targeting Shia Muslim in Quetta killing 89 people
2013	Police arrests and detains Malik Ishaque, the founder of militant group Lashkar-e—Jhangvi
March 24, 2013	Pervez Musharraf returns to Pakistan from exile to organize All Pakistan Muslim League (APML) and participate in May 11, 2013 elections

April 14, 2013   Dr. Tahirul Qadri calls for Dharna on May 11, 2013 in Islamabad as a protest to boycott the voting in election due to alleged conspiracy and fraud of elections Commission for not following the provisions of Article 62 and 63. He blamed all National Institutions as part of this conspiracy.